THE EVERYTHING.

GUIDE TO
WRITING CHILDREN'S BOOKS
2ND EDITION

Dear Reader,

My parents were storytellers. My father described in detail the pig that tried to gobble him down (nonfiction), and the adventures of a brother and sister, Jack and Tack (fiction). My mother inspired with a picture book about a little train engine, and later with books about the mysteries of deer and dogs and horses. I told my own children stories of a bullfrog who rescued a baby, and of an alabunny (half gator and half bunny) who saved the frozen swamp.

In my career as a professional writer, enthusiasm for children's stories has seemed to guide my pen. I have written books about children living in the woods, living in haunted houses, and even living on the moon!

Our daughter Eva entertained the family with stories of fairies; later she became my editor, and eventually my writing partner.

In this book we share what we have learned: how to capture your best ideas, develop them, and present them to the publishing world. Writing for children begins with stories in your heart. We help you bring those stories to life and share them with others.

Sincerely,

Luke Wallin and Eva Sage Gordon

Welcome to the EVERYTHING® Series!

These handy, accessible books give you all you need to tackle a difficult project, gain a new hobby, comprehend a fascinating topic, prepare for an exam, or even brush up on something you learned back in school but have since forgotten.

You can choose to read an *Everything®* book from cover to cover or just pick out the information you want from our four useful boxes: e-questions, e-facts, e-alerts, and e-ssentials.

We give you everything you need to know on the subject, but throw in a lot of fun stuff along the way, too.

We now have more than 400 *Everything®* books in print, spanning such wide-ranging categories as weddings, pregnancy, cooking, music instruction, foreign language, crafts, pets, New Age, and so much more. When you're done reading them all, you can finally say you know *Everything®*!

QUESTION

Answers to common questions

FACT

Important snippets of information

ALERT

Urgent warnings

ESSENTIAL

Quick handy tips

PUBLISHER Karen Cooper

DIRECTOR OF ACQUISITIONS AND INNOVATION Paula Munier

MANAGING EDITOR, EVERYTHING® SERIES Lisa Laing

COPY CHIEF Casey Ebert

ASSISTANT PRODUCTION EDITOR Jacob Erickson

ACQUISITIONS EDITOR Lisa Laing

DEVELOPMENT EDITOR Wendy Lazear

EDITORIAL ASSISTANT Ross Weisman

EVERYTHING® SERIES COVER DESIGNER Erin Alexander

LAYOUT DESIGNERS Colleen Cunningham, Elisabeth Lariviere, Ashley Vierra, Denise Wallace

Visit the entire Everything® series at *www.everything.com*

THE
EVERYTHING®
GUIDE TO
WRITING
CHILDREN'S BOOKS
2ND EDITION

How to write, publish, and promote books
for children of all ages!

Luke Wallin and Eva Sage Gordon
Foreword by Peter Abrahams

Avon, Massachusetts

Dedicated to Mary Elizabeth Gordon

An Everything® Series Book.
Everything® and everything.com® are registered trademarks of F+W Media, Inc.

Published by Adams Media, a division of F+W Media, Inc.
57 Littlefield Street, Avon, MA 02322 U.S.A.
www.adamsmedia.com

ISBN 10: 1-4405-0549-7
ISBN 13: 978-1-4405-0549-2
eISBN 10: 1-4405-0550-0
eISBN 13: 978-1-4405-0550-8

Printed in the United States of America.

10 9 8 7

Library of Congress Cataloging-in-Publication Data
Wallin, Luke.
The everything guide to writing children's books. — 2nd ed. / Luke Wallin and Eva Sage Gordon.
p. cm.
Rev. ed. of: The everything guide to writing children's books / Lesley Bolton. c2003.
Includes bibliographical references and index.
ISBN-13: 978-1-4405-0549-2 (alk. paper)
ISBN-10: 1-4405-0549-7 (alk paper)
ISBN-13: 978-1-4405-0550-8 (e-book)
ISBN-10: 1-4405-0550-0 (e-book)
1. Children's literature—Authorship. I. Gordon, Eva S., 1986- II. Bolton, Lesley. Everything guide to writing
children's books. III. Title.
PN147.5.B65   2011
808.06'8—dc22   2010039121

This publication is designed to provide accurate and authoritative information with regard to the subject matter covered. It is sold with the understanding that the publisher is not engaged in rendering legal, accounting, or other professional advice. If legal advice or other expert assistance is required, the services of a competent professional person should be sought.

—From a *Declaration of Principles* jointly adopted by a Committee of the
American Bar Association and a Committee of Publishers and Associations

Many of the designations used by manufacturers and sellers to distinguish their products are claimed as trademarks. Where those designations appear in this book and Adams Media was aware of a trademark claim, the designations have been printed with initial capital letters.

This book is available at quantity discounts for bulk purchases.
For information, please call 1-800-289-0963.

Contents

Acknowledgments

Luke thanks:

My insightful colleagues in the Writing for Children and Young Adults track at Spalding University's MFA program: Louella Bryant, Joyce McDonald, and Susan Campbell Bartoletti. Lucille Penner for sharing secrets of writing nonfiction for children. My children and grandchildren for providing me with an endless treasure trove of stories.

Eva thanks:

Neil Gordon for welcoming me to the writing program at The New School University, and for talking to me about writing and publishing whenever I knocked on his office door. Kristy Davis for reminding me that writing books is a goal worth striving for, and that reading books is good for you. Also for cake. My brother and sister-in-law, Clay and Sarah Wallin, for lending me their house to write in over Christmas week 2009. Scott Mendel for introducing me to the business of book publishing from an agent's point of view.

Luke and Eva would both like to thank:

Our Acquisitions Editor, Lisa Laing, at Adams Media, for her speedy question-answering and assistance at every stage in the process; our attentive and helpful agent Katelynn Lacopo for bringing this project to us and for making herself available throughout its completion; Lloyd Kelly, Jr., for inspiration, ideas, and friendship; Sena Jeter Naslund for guidance and wisdom; and Mary Elizabeth Gordon for ongoing life support.

Top Ten Tips for
Writing Children's Books

1. Create characters you truly love, hate, admire, and fear.

2. Tell stories you yearn to tell: feel the desire of your protagonist to reach a goal; fear the obstacles blocking that path; show the details of the struggle.

3. Choose small events in the world you know, or large events on the world stage, to inspire your stories. The key is that they speak to you, and move you.

4. Read, read, read—read books written for the target age group, set in your chosen historical period, and of the type of book you want to write.

5. Try writing for different age groups, and in different voices. You will discover your niche through writing, not by thinking about writing.

6. Expect to make mistakes in the beginning—everyone does. Look for constructive feedback from people who know good writing.

7. Protect yourself from negative people: show your work only to trusted friends, or professional writing teachers or coaches.

8. As soon as you have received an offer on your first manuscript, but before you have signed a contract, join the Author's Guild and ask them for assistance.

9. Organize your life to become a writer: keep good files and maintain a disciplined work schedule; capture your dreams, reveries, and inspired moments in notebooks.

10. Try out new ideas all the time, edit your work patiently, and send it out steadily.

Foreword

I'd written fifteen crime fiction novels before tackling my first young adult novel, *Down the Rabbit Hole*, Book One in the Echo Falls series. I was lucky in three ways. First, and probably least helpful to readers of this excellent guide, was the fact that I was invited to give it a try by a wonderful editor at a major children's publisher. She'd read a book of mine called *The Tutor* in which a ten-year-old girl plays a supporting role and she thought a children's mystery series could be built around a similar character. The editor and I had a thirty-minute chat in her Manhattan office and then I got in my car and headed home. Approaching the first rest stop on I-95, I felt a craving for fries, and during that little pit stop the main elements of *Down the Rabbit Hole* came to me. Those out-of-the-blue experiences are the very best—and rarest—things about what my grandmother used to call "the writing game."

Second stroke of luck: I had four kids of my own, an endless mine of material. I'd seen it all! At the time, my youngest daughter was a thirteen-year-old eighth grader, just like Ingrid Levin-Hill, amateur detective and star of the Echo Falls series. My daughter read the manuscript chapter by chapter during the writing process, as did my wife. My wife, probably as you or I would do, made tentative pencil marks on the pages, and not too many. My daughter, on the other hand, used ink, and commented plenty, changing dialogue and slashing away with gusto. Ingrid turned out to be that way, too. I wonder why.

Third, I quickly discovered that I loved writing for children. Writing is challenging and sometimes lonely work, and I can't imagine doing it in the absence of true love on the writer's part. In this case, I transported myself every writing day (which means just about every day for me—okay, not Thanksgiving) back to the special world of childhood, an endlessly fresh and fascinating period when the world is engaged for the first time in all its good and bad. I've come to believe that we're somewhat like trees, with the rings of each year hidden inside. I found the thirteen-year-old ring within me to be very accessible, and urge anyone interested in writing for children to spend some time seriously contemplating their younger selves. Just as you can work to improve your literary techniques, you can also work to improve your imagination.

People always ask what I did to adjust to the younger readership. The answer is: nothing. Whether you're writing in the first person or any of the variants of the third person, if you really get into the heads of your characters then the vocabulary, syntax, thought patterns, and attitude will magically come out right. And if not, revise! And again and again and again! Still loving the job? Then this book is for you.

—Peter Abrahams

Introduction

THERE ARE THREE THINGS you must do to become a writer of children's books, whether fiction or nonfiction. First, you must write. Second, you must revise. Third, you must send your work out. Sometimes writers concentrate on one or two of these activities and neglect the third. Not you! You've taken the first step to becoming a real children's author—you bought this book!

Writing fiction, whether for children or adults, begins with story ideas. Sometimes these ideas come in dreams, on an airplane, when you're listening to music, or when you're singing in the shower—moments when you are free of other people, responsibilities, and distractions. Your mind floats a little, drifts a little, and you picture an image, a character, a crazy rhyme, or a line of dialogue that makes you smile. Most people let these reveries go, and they are lost forever. Not you! As a writer, you will capture these rhymes, dreams, and images by jotting them down in a small note-book that you keep close at hand. This is the first step in working with your subconscious mind. All literature comes from this hidden source—not just children's literature.

As a writer for children, you won't limit your jottings to the beautiful, harmonic, or joyful. While there is much pleasure in the music of writing, and in creating attractive characters, settings, and adventures, children's literature has a dark side, too. Think of Alice's fear of the Red Queen, or Harry Potter's terror of his nemesis Voldemort.

Children's literature is rooted in oral storytelling for both children and adults, and much of that storytelling was practiced to help people survive real challenges. Think of the stories collected in eighteenth-century Europe, tales such as "Jack and the Beanstalk" and "Little Red Riding Hood." Do you think the giant who threatened Jack, and the wolf that threatened Red Riding Hood, represented real dangers in the world of eighteenth-century children? Or do you think those scary figures represented anxieties and insecurities—the inner demons of children who feel powerless much of the time?

Scholars argue each side of this, but *writers* know that stories of conflict between good and evil characters serve *both* purposes for children.

Through good books, young readers learn to cope with threatening forces in the world around them, and within themselves.

Just as you will capture joyful moments in your notebook, so you may capture difficult experiences that will be equally useful in your writing. An unreasonable male boss, for example, cast into fiction as a nosy female neighbor, could allow you the freedom to use feelings of anger creatively. You could bring to life a memorable foe who loses out in the end. How satisfying, for both writer and reader!

If you want to write nonfiction books for children, jot down reminders of those moments when experiencing something new or learning a piece of information held special interest for you: cactus flowers that grow in the desert, foxes that live in the city, or stars that turn into black holes. Your curiosity and love of detail can lead to learning the sequences of cause and effect which led to these fascinating facts, and how they became known. This research can lead you to write true stories of natural science, history, and biography for children. What budding artist wouldn't like to read about a young Georgia O'Keeffe? What future scientist wouldn't want to learn about a rare Florida Panther and its Everglades home?

Do you dream of writing both fiction and nonfiction for children? Which do you think you would be better at? What age readers might you have a special knack for engaging? Here's an important secret: you mustn't just think about it. You must actually try it!

Begin with an experiment. Write the first paragraph (and if that goes well, the first page). Try different contexts for your ideas: a picture book, then a middle-grade novel, and then a serious young adult story. Try incorporating different elements in your story: realism, history, humor, and fantasy. Try writing an opening to your story in the voice of your main character; now try writing the same opening in the voice of an observer, or "third person" narrator. You will surprise and delight yourself with these experiments.

Above all else, you must write! What about revision and sending out your work? Don't worry, we'll get there. First, find the notebook and the pen, and *start writing*!

CHAPTER 1

The Importance of Children's Books

Children's books teach and entertain, offer adventure and escape, and comfort children with the knowledge that they are not alone in the world. Do you remember reading a book as a kid and thinking "This is amazing. This character is just like me"? Childhood can be a confusing time, and children are helped tremendously when they learn that other people have felt the joys and concerns they feel. The children's books you write can have a lasting impact on the lives of readers.

A Brief History

Today's children's book writer can strengthen her work by understanding the history of the form. The art of storytelling has been passed down for generations—and so have the steps writers have taken to make books appealing to children.

Oral Tradition

People told stories for centuries before writing was invented. Children's books, like adult books, emerged from these oral traditions. The art of storytelling was highly regarded (even as a profession at times), and stories were passed down to children from their parents, traveling bards, and elders of the community or tribe.

Every culture has used storytelling to pass on traditions and beliefs to future generations, as well as to explain the mysteries of nature, convey history, influence values, and entertain. Tales had to be told in such a way that they would be remembered. Storytellers often performed their stories and sometimes brought along drawings to help illustrate the tale. Occasionally, they would embellish or alter a common story to keep the attention of the audience.

Storytellers required a certain knack for sizing up an audience. They had to recognize the needs and wants of those listening and figure out a suitable approach. They also had to alter their techniques according to the type of audience, whether it was adults only, children only, adults and children combined, or people of a different community, town, or tribe. All these factors had to be considered before and *during* a story performance.

It is important to recognize and respect the oral tradition. Though sometimes thought a thing of the past, it is valuable to writers of today—especially authors of children's books. As you progress in your writing, you will find that having an audience will help to hone your skills as a performer of your work. And just as the tellers of so long ago sized up their audiences, so will you.

Each of the following steps comes from the oral storytelling tradition. Taking them will improve your writing.

- As you compose and revise, read your stories aloud to yourself. Pretend you are reading on the radio, and speak slowly and clearly, with feeling. Test the sound of sentences, improve rhythm, eliminate awkward phrases, and shape realistic dialogue.

- When you have completed a draft, read it aloud to children of the appropriate age. Note which parts hold them and which parts don't.
- When you read a story to a child, you are carrying forward the great oral tradition. Meditate on the values and memories you wish to impart to the next generation. What has changed since you were younger? What do kids need to hear from your unique perspective?

Incorporating these tips from the oral tradition will strengthen both your writing and your presentation of your stories.

FACT

The ancient Greek myths are a good example of how oral tradition promotes the longevity of a story. Had these myths not been so entertaining and recounted in such a compelling way, they would not have survived long enough to be written down.

Books for Children

Before the seventeenth century, most of the literature available to children had been published for adults. Children relished the tales of Robin Hood and King Arthur—exciting stories that featured dashing heroes matched against terrible foes. These stories introduced children to big ideas of the adult world. Robin Hood worked for justice, robbing the rich to feed the poor; King Arthur fought corruption and foreign invasion.

The first books written especially for children featured none of these things. Instead, these books were packed with pages of advice. *The Book of Curtesye* by William Caxton (published in 1477) contained instructions such as "Don't undo your girdle at the table." It wasn't until John Newbery published *A Little Pretty Pocket Book* in 1744 that entertainment became a valued component of literature for children. Its subtitle read, in part, "with two letters from Jack the Giant Killer." Newbery's books reached heights of popularity and soon other publishers began to follow suit.

The nineteenth century brought about a flowering of illustrators, and new printing capabilities allowed for color illustrations. In America, Scribners published a magazine that was designed specifically for children called *St. Nicholas Magazine.*

Soon thereafter, librarians began building collections of children's books. They set out on a mission to persuade publishers that there was a market for quality books with illustrations that would appeal to children. Their dedication paid off, and in 1921 Macmillan opened the first department solely for trade children's books. Other publishers opened their own departments once it was determined that children's publishing was a profitable enterprise.

QUESTION

Is the Newbery Medal named after John Newbery?
Yes. The Newbery Medal, awarded every year for the best children's book, was established in 1921 by the American Library Association in honor of the famous publisher and bookseller.

Children's publishing snowballed. Today, children's publishing is big business and there is a huge market of eager children (and their parents) out there just waiting to be satisfied. There are three enduring qualities in children's books today:

- They feature adventure and excitement.
- Their heroes are clever and moral, while their villains are clever and immoral.
- They are built on big ideas, such as justice and freedom.

Writing for today's children means exactly what it did years ago: incorporating dramatic elements into your work in order to capture and hold readers. Children's books share with oral storytelling the devices of showing character through action, building tension, and revealing events.

The Mission

There are a number of reasons why people write for children. Every writer has stories to tell. The purpose of children's books—at the most rudimentary level—is to teach or to entertain. That said, the best children's writing contains a writer's unique voice. It is likely that all three of these purposes will be a part of your overall mission.

Writing for Self-Expression

Stories that are memorable—that engage deep feelings, not just thoughts, in readers—are those *you* are burning to uncover and tell. You will find satisfaction in writing if you explore the stories most meaningful to you. Many writers for adults and children have said that their crucial material came from their own lives up until the age of twelve. The great thing about writing fiction is that you can change these stories any way you like—you can transform people into animals, or create composite characters out of several remembered people.

When you write about real events, whether from your own or someone else's life, try not to make your stories too depressing. You can paint a difficult situation—for example, of the WWII Holocaust or the Cherokee Trail of Tears—but do it in a measured way; use short scenes and chapters rather than long ones; build anticipation for possible escape and solution, but *not* for the sake of making your reader wallow in misery. Remember that your purpose is to connect with a child. Becoming a successful writer also requires that you pay attention to your audience—this means not just children but also the adults who will buy your book. They will be looking for stories that teach various subjects, entertain, promote literacy, and inspire creativity and imagination. As you write, consider each of these goals of your customers.

ESSENTIAL

If you are interested in helping a child learn to read, consider writing easy reader books. These books are designed specifically for the child who is beginning to read on his own.

Writing to Teach

Children are hungry for knowledge. Their capacity for learning is tremendous. Children's authors often set out to help educate children about topics the writers feel are important.

In the past, many children's books were produced to teach manners and good behavior, to inform children about their culture's present and past, or to school children in religious beliefs. While these types of books still exist, the variety of topics available to children has expanded considerably.

Nowadays, books are often designed to help children see what lies outside their own world and understand what's changing within it. You can easily find books that teach children about racism, sexuality, war, disease, divorce, and death. Books about the differences between people are important to prepare children for events in their lives. Today in the United States, the average person moves every few years, and the divorce rate is high. Editors and parents know that personal changes will confront many children with new social and cultural realities. Books about diversity can promote tolerance among children. The more they know about other communities, the better chance they stand of growing into well-rounded, successful, and happy adults.

Of course, there are also books about love, friendship, peace, and strength. With the thousands of topics available, children can discover for themselves where their interests lie. The hope is that one topic of interest will lead to another, which will lead to another, and so on.

Writing to Entertain

Although books intended to teach a valuable lesson are well and good, everyone needs a little fun—especially kids. If you haven't noticed, children can have a very short attention span. Children are usually straightforward and honest (especially when it comes to their likes and dislikes), and don't have to bend to niceties as adults often do. If a child is bored, he will let you know. A good children's book can make all the difference between a squirming child and an attentive child.

Some children's books are designed solely to entertain or amuse. Often these books will have a rhyming or otherwise lulling language that amuses, calms, or comforts a child. Sometimes they are used to divert a child's attention from a disappointment, such as not being able to play outside while it's raining. They will keep a child busy having fun in not-so-fun places such as the doctor's office. And let's not forget, some are just meant to tell a good story.

For those who argue that books designed solely for entertainment have no value, think again. If those books grab the attention of a child and spark an interest in reading, what greater value is there? Entertainment, whether on its own or combined with instruction, is an important quality that children's books possess.

Additional Benefits

Children's books are loaded with additional benefits that supplement the purposes of expressing yourself, teaching, and entertaining. You should be aware of far-reaching impacts your books may have. Some of these influences may help to motivate you when you are tempted throw up your hands.

Promoting Literacy

One of the most important benefits of a book is promoting literacy. Let's face it, those who are able to read and write have an easier go of things in this world than those who are illiterate. Every book, whether or not it was designed specifically for this purpose, can help a child to grasp language and literacy. If a child is able to derive pleasure and perhaps satisfy curiosity from a book at a young age, that child is more likely to make books a part of his life. Those who read extensively are often good writers, have a strong vocabulary, are able to communicate effectively, and have sound grammar and spelling skills.

FACT

In the 1980s, the concept of "whole language" was introduced. This approach encouraged the use of literature in all subjects, not just reading classes. As a result, trade books were brought into schools to replace some textbooks and to encourage an interest in reading. For example, if a class is studying World War II, then a historical novel based on that war might be introduced to the class.

Learning to Listen

Listening is hard—even adults have difficulty with it. Listening is different from hearing. It is a very important skill that takes practice and patience.

While hearing is simply the process of registering sound through the ear, listening requires active participation in comprehending what is being heard. Children will develop good listening skills if they are read to on a regular basis, especially if starting off at a very young age. By helping to strengthen their listening skills, you are also helping them to become better communicators.

Inspiring Creativity and Imagination

If you've ever had contact with children, you know that they are naturally creative and can sometimes have wild imaginations. Since it seems like just part of their charm, many of us take their creativity for granted. As children grow older, outside influences can stifle creativity, and they can find themselves as adults wondering where their imaginations have fled. Books can help to continuously inspire and promote creativity. By introducing new ideas, a book will stimulate the mind to go off on tangents, creating a cycle of original thought.

A Healthy Escape

Just like adults, children sometimes need a form of escapism to take a breather from the trials of life. Children are very perceptive and can feel the strain of tense situations even if they are not able to fully express these feelings. With all of the harmful forms of escapism available to children today, books should be made available as a healthy choice for distraction. Books can transport the reader to a different time and place, leaving behind the present and all its troubles.

A Child's World

Children's books are most often bought by adults. Because you will want your books to appeal to an adult's sensibility, it is sometimes easy to allow yourself to be swayed by an adult's viewpoint when writing. What you must keep in mind is that ultimately children's books are for children, regardless of who buys them. It is this quality that makes books so important to the children themselves. Books can become a secret treasure. Children can explore their own tastes and interests through the books they choose to read. If they feel as though a book was written and designed just for them, children will create a bond with the literature. So, write children's books for children.

To write for children, you need to acknowledge their view of the world, which can be quite different from that of an adult. Reading child psychology can be helpful. You have two excellent resources at your fingertips: your memories and children themselves. We'll get into the specifics of writing for children later in the book. For right now, get to know them.

Using Your Memory

The memories from your own childhood are a good place to start. Start off with a description of yourself at a particular age that you can see most clearly. Sketch out a brief character description including things such as your age, hair color, eye color, height, weight, clothing preferences, hobbies, friends, where you lived, and general likes and dislikes.

Next, write down a timeline of significant events during your childhood. Leave some space because one memory may spark another and you might want to go back and add something. Once you are satisfied with your timeline, take each event individually and retell the story in first person—but try to tell it as you would have immediately following its occurrence. Use the character description to get you going; how old were you and what did you look like during this event? Then go on to describe how you felt, what your reactions were, and what you observed. Complete this exercise for each event. You will probably find that the more stories you retell, the easier they are to describe from a child's point of view.

ESSENTIAL

If you are having trouble remembering specifics from your childhood, take a look at an old photo album. Pictures can trigger memories and even provide details that have long been forgotten. They may also inspire future stories.

A child's view is quite different from that of an adult, and a child's priorities differ from an adult's. Remember that a child is short, physically weak, politically powerless, limited in knowledge, and lacking experiences that could allow processing information in a mature way. All these factors will influence how a child responds to your work.

While a security blanket may be the most important thing in the world to a child, an adult may look at it as just another piece of cloth. As you try to recapture a child's view, take these observations into consideration and use your own memories to help gain a better understanding of children and their world.

Being a Spy

One of the best ways to get to know children is to watch them. If you have children of your own, this is a great place to start, but don't limit yourself to a select few. (Plus, your own children will most likely take more notice of your presence, and their behavior may be influenced by it.) If at all possible, study large groups of children. Pay close attention to what they say, how they interact with each other and adults, what they take an interest in, and their body language.

Consider yourself on a covert operation. Try to stay out of sight as much as possible. This doesn't mean you have to hide in a nearby bush; just keep out of the way and don't stare blatantly. Even if you don't know the children you are studying, the mere presence of an adult (especially a stranger) will sometimes affect they way they behave.

If you work with children, the covert operation should be an easy one. However, if you aren't normally around kids, or want to study a different group, it may be a little more difficult to seek out children. The following are some good places to start:

- Parks
- Community or school playgrounds
- Organized playgroups
- Church youth groups
- Sports events
- Carnivals or fairs
- Libraries

Keep a notebook with you and jot down your observations, even if they don't seem to have any significance. If you are close enough to hear conversations, write them down word for word—it just may help you with dialogue when it comes time to write your story.

ALERT

When observing children, be sure to let the supervising adults know what you are doing. Your presence may seem suspicious and cause alarm. If you explain your presence your intentions won't be misconstrued.

If you are unable to observe children firsthand or would like additional resources, you may want to consider reading books and magazines on parenting. These references will help you to understand the physical and emotional milestones of a child's growth process.

Not Just Books Anymore

Children's books are important for reading purposes, of course, but they also inspire movies and television shows. This can be good and it can be bad, depending on how you look at it. Blockbuster movies and hit television series will certainly raise awareness of the book. As an author, you will be able to reach a wider audience—both the children who have already read your book and those who haven't. Some children who see the story acted out for them may not bother reading the book, but then there are also those children who love the story so much that they beg their parents to take them to the bookstore immediately. It works both ways.

Harry Potter and *Twilight*

When the first Harry Potter book was published back in 1997, J. K. Rowling was an unknown writer. The first book, *Harry Potter and the Sorcerer's Stone,* was an unexpected hit, but the movie adaptation of it, and of the subsequent books, grew the awareness of Rowling and the book series to new heights. Now millions of people all over the world are reading Harry Potter books. A similar thing has happened with the *Twilight* series. Stephenie Meyer was a stay-at-home mom who dreamed up the

Twilight story (literally!), and after hastily writing a 500-page draft, she sent out query letters to agents and publishers. Six months later, she was looking at a three-book deal with Little, Brown, one of the largest Young Adult (YA) publishers in the business. Soon after that, the movie versions of the series were hitting theaters. Both Harry Potter and *Twilight* are examples of books receiving more attention (and more readers) as a result of their film adaptations.

FACT

Many original movies and television shows inspire children's books. Often these books will be published in series form as "novelizations" of original episodes, or continue the story line of a television show such as *Full House* or *Buffy the Vampire Slayer*.

One negative side of having your children's or YA book adapted for the screen is that producers will usually need to alter stories, either to fit within specific time allotments or to appeal to more diverse audiences. Another possibility is that the film will overshadow the book, as in the case of many Disney movies. Walt Disney knew what he was doing when he brought *Snow White, Cinderella, Sleeping Beauty, Beauty and the Beast*, and others to life onscreen. These animated features have become classics—and although many children know the stories are based on old fairy tales, the Walt Disney adaptations dominate the cultural imagination. The original books are a footnote to the movies.

Advancements in Technology

Some people are of the opinion that advancements in technology are going to cause the extinction of the book. This fear is not new; over the years, newly emerged technologies such as television, videos, video games, computers, and the Internet have pushed the panic buttons of publishers and writers alike. While these technologies have risen in popularity, and while e-books have made a splash in the book market, the printed children's book has, so far, stood its ground.

People still have a close relationship with printed books. The ability to scribble in the margins, highlight passages, dog-ear pages, and feel the paper between your fingers as you build the anticipation of turning the page are sentimental qualities that aren't soon to be forgotten. How many times have you opened a new book and taken a big whiff? How many times have you scanned someone's bookshelf for something good to read and picked out a book that was well-worn? Printed books will always hold a special place in readers' hearts, despite the growing popularity of e-readers. And even when e-books begin to outsell print, the book market will still hold its ground. Don't forget, e-books need writers, too.

CHAPTER 2

Types of Children's Books

Because children's books span such a wide age and reading-level range—infants to teenagers—there have to be distinct divisions that break them down into smaller categories. For example, a twelve-year-old may prefer reading about a thirteen- or fourteen-year old protagonist to one who is ten years old. In other respects, such as complexity of language, books about these two ages may be similar. This is one illustration of the fine line between middle grade and young adult. This chapter will outline the different types of children's books.

The Standard Categories

The two standard categories of books are fiction and nonfiction. At the heart of fiction is a story; at the heart of nonfiction is fact. Before you begin writing, you will need to decide if you are going to write fiction, nonfiction, or both. From there, you will decide which types of children's books and reading levels suit you.

Fiction

Fiction reveals truths. How is this possible? As your made-up characters interact with each other, overcoming obstacles and striving to reach their goals, you will sense whether their actions and words are honest and accurate. So will your readers. Writers often report that their fictional people seem alive; part of the writer's job is to listen to what the characters want to say, rather than force words upon them.

When publishers seek good fiction, they mean honestly explored stories of made-up people who live in the world we all share; the stories will contain joys and problems of real people—love, jealousy, greed, ambition, and so on. Even fantasy and science fiction stories reflect these dynamics of our experience.

Children's fiction can also explore alternate worlds. The best science fiction and fantasy stories offer readers the fun of an imagined universe while illuminating the world we live in. Characters may live in star ships or graveyards yet represent people in normal settings. You may choose to retell the story of Snow White, but you will be using a folk tale to say something about the relationships in real families.

Fiction comes in many different genres: fairy tales, folk tales, myths, romantic fiction, historical fiction, fantasy, ghost stories, science fiction, westerns, adventure stories, and horror, to name a few. For each of these genres, there is a particular kind of fictional world, just as there are writers and readers who love to visit there, and publishers looking for these kinds of stories. So choose the world that attracts you, and start writing down ideas for characters and story lines in that setting.

Try writing the first page of a book of one of the types listed above. There is a particular kind of emotion associated with each category, and by experimenting you will discover which ones you have the most feeling for. When you reach the end of that first page, if you feel drawn to keep writing, you may have begun an exciting journey. Try this in the voice of a character, then start over and try it in a third person narrative voice.

Nonfiction

Though nonfiction must stick to the facts, it must also be lively. You can find ways to make facts, and the theories that help explain them, appealing to children. Sports, science, history, geography, nature, cooking, biography, evolution, and health are just a few of the topics that can be explored in children's books.

In addition to the endless subjects available, there are different approaches you can take to presenting them. Maybe you would like to create a documentary-style book about the Pony Express, or tell the story of how bees find flowers and report back to the hive. Nearly any activity can be transformed into a how-to book. For example, if you know your way around a kitchen, you could write a how-to book on vegetarian meals to cook with children.

ESSENTIAL

You already have a wealth of information at your fingertips if you decide to write about what you know. But do research your topic; while you may think you know everything already, you'll want to verify your information and be up-to-date on advancements.

If you believe you would like to write nonfiction, think about your own activities and interests. What is your occupation? Where did you grow up? Is there a subject you'd like to learn more about? What are your hobbies? Use the answers to these questions as starting points for your compilation of ideas.

Whether you decide to write fiction or nonfiction, you will need to decide what you want your book to look like and what reading level you want to address. Let's take a look at five types of children's books and the reading levels appropriate to each one.

Picture Books

When speaking of children's books, most people have picture books in mind. These are the books that combine illustrations with text. They are the books that are read at bedtime, during story hour at the library, in kindergarten classes, and by older siblings to younger ones. They mark the beginning of a child's love of literature.

At most bookstores, picture books take up a good portion of the children's department. They are popular with both children and adults. Kids browse the bookshelves looking at the lively illustrations and stunning colors. Parents browse the bookshelves looking for a story that will be a pleasure to read over and over again to their children. Some adults love to give picture books as gifts—to people of all ages.

FACT

Picture books are usually rather short, which is ideal for the short attention spans of children. However, there are many successful picture books that tell longer stories and are text-heavy.

The Design

Picture books are normally between twenty-four and thirty-two pages long. These page counts include the front matter (copyright page, title page, dedication, and acknowledgment pages). For example, a thirty-two page picture book minus the front matter may leave only twenty-eight pages for the story.

Word counts for picture books normally range between 200 and 1,500 words. There are exceptions. Some picture books have very small illustrations, leaving room for a lot of text. Others have no words at all.

To help you write within the structure of picture books, try breaking up your text into pages. The first page of your story will normally be on the right-hand page, so it will stand alone. Pages 2 and 3 will be a two-page spread so a small cliffhanger should occur on the odd-numbered pages throughout.

You will want to envision *provisional* illustrations that may accompany your text, but keep in mind that the illustrator will contribute a special vision to this partnership.

Enough action in the text should take place on each page to allow for an illustration. On the other hand, you don't want too much action because there might not be room to illustrate it all. A page of picture-book text should *gently suggest* visual ideas, but not specify them in detail. Let the illustrator's imagination have freedom to roam.

Writing Picture Books

First of all, let's do away with a common misconception: You do not have to be able to illustrate to write and sell picture books. And unless you are a professional illustrator, do not submit drawings with your text. Check out Chapter 9 for more information about illustrators.

While picture books are easy to read and love, they are not easy to write. Yes, the text may be quite simple and short, but that is misleading. Because space is limited in picture books, every single word must be very carefully chosen; you simply don't have the room to take your time with the story. Plus, the writer must take into consideration the illustrations. Type out the text of several picture books you admire. This will give you a sense of the writer's job, as opposed to the illustrator's job.

ESSENTIAL

Talk to a children's librarian and find out which picture books are most popular with children. Then ask which picture books are most popular with adults. You will most likely find that there are differences in which books adults like to read over and over and which books children like to hear over and over.

Children typically have short attention spans. If you want to capture their interest, your text should be constantly moving. Every page should contain action, including the very first page. Don't spend precious space setting up the story, just dive right in. You want to capture the child's attention from the get-go. Plus, you'll keep his attention by including small cliffhangers that motivate him to turn the page. Just as novels leave you wanting to read more with the end of each chapter, picture books leave you with that desire at the end of each spread.

Types of Picture Books

When you browse the bookshelves for picture books, you'll notice several different types. The most common has a large illustration accompanied by a few lines of text on each page. Not every story works best in this format. There are a few other types of picture books you might try writing:

- **Board or baby books.** These books are built to stand up to the destructive tendencies of babies and toddlers. They are often made of cardboard and are usually sixteen pages long with an illustration accompanied by only a couple of words per page.
- **Wordless picture books.** Just as the name implies, these picture books do not have text. The illustrations tell the story by themselves.
- **Novelty books.** These books have an additional element that make the book interactive or otherwise entertaining. Some novelty books have pop-ups, pull tabs, graduated page lengths, holes in the pages, or accessories that complement the story.
- **Concept books.** These books focus on one concept and don't necessarily have to tell a story. Whether the topic is something tangible or visible, such as colors, or something more complex or psychological, such as overcoming a fear of the dark, a concept book will explore its concept in whatever format suits it best.

EXAMPLES OF PICTURE BOOKS
- *Where the Wild Things Are* by Maurice Sendak
- *Goodnight Moon* by Margaret Wise Brown
- *The Snowy Day* by Ezra Jack Keats
- *Blueberries for Sal* by Robert McCloskey
- *Corduroy* by Don Freeman
- *The Velveteen Rabbit* by Margery Williams
- *The Tale of Peter Rabbit* by Beatrix Potter
- *Owl Moon* by Jane Yolen
- *The Girl Who Loved Wild Horses* by Paul Goble
- *Wild in the City* by Jan Thornhill

If you want to write picture books, spend some time at a bookstore or library and take a look at the structure and style of the picture books available. Ask the salesperson or librarian which picture books are popular and look closely at these (but remember that this information might be different in another location). Also, spend time with books that seem boring or unappealing and try to pinpoint why you *don't* like them. The more time you can spend in the current children's book market, the better you will get to know what does and does not work.

Early Readers

Children learning to read may start off with picture books, often because that is what they are accustomed to and that's what is lying around the house. However, as they progress, their self-confidence is heightened. They are proud of their "big kid" abilities and start to look down on "baby books." This is where early readers step in.

Because children learn so quickly, not much time is spent in this transitional phase of reading. However, this does not diminish the importance of early readers. These books are valuable stepping stones that will promote a child's enthusiasm and comprehension.

The Design

Early readers are books designed specifically for children who are learning to read. The books are usually taller and not as wide as picture books. They have a more grown-up, sophisticated feel that children love. But they aren't so sophisticated that they overwhelm a child. The books normally use large type and the spacing between the lines is increased to allow for more white space on a page.

ESSENTIAL

A few publishing companies have word lists that need to be used by authors for their books. If you admire a particular publisher of early readers and are determined to be published by that company, you should check its website for submission guidelines, in case there is a vocabulary list you must use.

Although not classified as picture books, early readers do have illustrations. Whereas picture books rely on the illustrations to help the viewer capture the story, early readers focus on the words to secure the story, using illustrations to provide prompts for the reader while enhancing the entertainment.

These books vary in page lengths and word counts. Typically an early reader is forty-eight to sixty-four pages long, with some of the simpler books being thirty-two pages. The word counts are comparable to picture books, though they normally shoot for the higher end of around 1,500 words.

Writing Early Readers

When writing early readers you must keep in mind that while they are for older children, the text can't be as complex as some picture books. Picture books are most often read by adults to children and can make use of an extended vocabulary and sentence structure. Although early readers should have simple text, this does not mean that you should avoid big words. Children are smart and crave knowledge. If you fill an early reader with very simple words, a child may feel that her intelligence is insulted.

Don't be afraid to throw in a big word here and there if it helps promote the story. However, if you do use a word that children may not have heard before, try to use it again somewhere in the story. Of course you don't want to go overboard and have that same word on every page, nor do you want to riddle the story with complicated vocabulary. Find a good balance that will help a child to learn but not frustrate and discourage her.

While early readers can help strengthen a child's vocabulary, this is not the time or place to delve into advanced sentence structures. Keep the sentences simple and concise. Short and snappy text will give the book a rhythm and progression that a child can handle.

The plot, also, must be simple. Use a single, uncomplicated concept or problem and focus on its development. Avoid unnecessary detail. Like picture books, the story must be constantly moving. Use action, dialogue, and rich language to keep the story going. If you allow the story to idle for too long, a child will get bored and put down the book. Children can be unmerciful critics, and if you don't keep their attention at all times, you may lose their favor.

EXAMPLES OF EARLY READERS
- *Are You My Mother?* by P. D. Eastman
- *The Cat in the Hat* by Dr. Seuss
- *Little Bear* by Else Holmelund Minarik
- *Chester* by Syd Hoff
- *Frog and Toad* series by Arnold Lobel
- *Arthur's Prize Reader* by Lillian Hoban

Chapter Books

Chapter books are the next step up for a developing reader. These books welcome those who are getting bored with the early readers and are ready to advance their reading level. A chapter book should be relatively simple in story line, language, and sentence structure, but it should also be something of a challenge.

The Design

Chapter books, like early readers, are designed to give the book a "grown-up" feel. While the exterior of the book may look a lot like early readers, the interior is a bit different. Early readers have a lot of white space, which is welcoming to a child just learning to read on his own. When the child reaches the level of chapter books, he won't be as intimidated by lines of text. Therefore, the text of chapter books is usually a little smaller than that of early readers, and there isn't as much space between lines. Chapter books usually have some illustrations, but the story doesn't rely on them to help the reader along.

The story is broken down into several small chapters, paving the way for longer chapters in middle-grade books. Because these books have more text and generally more pages than early readers, the completion of each chapter gives the child a sense of satisfaction while not pressuring him to finish the entire book in one sitting.

Chapter books are normally between forty-eight and eighty pages long, though there are certainly those that are longer. Obviously, word counts (between 1,500 and 10,000) are going to be boosted since more text can fit on a page and there are fewer illustrations.

Writing Chapter Books

When writing chapter books, you should keep the plot simple, focusing on one specific concept or problem. The plots are usually centered on an experience children are familiar with. Children, at this stage in particular, like to relate to the stories they are reading. Using a setting that is recognizable and making the hero or heroine of the story a child are both good ways to capture the interest of your reader.

ESSENTIAL

When you are learning to distinguish between categories of children's books, the best way is to read a number of them from each category. You may want to pay special attention to the award-winners from the last ten years.

The story needs to be full of action. Each chapter should include an action episode that helps the story along. Children in this age group still get restless very easily. Every single sentence should hook the reader and the easiest way to accomplish this is to make sure something is happening on every page.

Kids love humor. If at all possible, definitely use humor in your story. Because chapter books most often portray common childhood experiences, humor can help a child to make light of situations that might normally be humiliating or grim. However, be careful with your use of humor; you don't want to turn everything into a joke, nor do you want to make fun of children.

EXAMPLES OF CHAPTER BOOKS

- *Sarah, Plain and Tall* by Patricia MacLachlan
- *Pippi Longstocking* by Astrid Lindgren
- *Ramona the Pest* by Beverly Cleary
- *Goosebumps* series by R. L. Stine
- *Baby-Sitters Little Sister* series by Ann M. Martin
- *The Secret of the Attic* by Sheri Cooper Sinykin
- *Because of Winn-Dixie* by Kate DiCamillo
- *The Borrowers* by Mary Norton

- *Heidi* by Johanna Spyri
- *Roll of Thunder, Hear My Cry* by Mildred D. Taylor

Hi-Lo Books

Another category of children's books is the hi-lo (high interest/low reading level) category. These books are designed for older children who are reading below their grade level. They want books that will explore their interests, but need books that are simpler in structure and vocabulary. Hi-lo books offer a compromise that makes learning to read an enjoyable experience.

EXAMPLES OF HI-LO BOOKS FOR YOUNGER READERS
- *The Barn* by Avi
- *Tales of a Fourth Grade Nothing* by Judy Blume
- *The Pinballs* by Betsy Byars
- *The Prince of the Pond* by Donna Jo Napoli

EXAMPLES OF HI-LO BOOKS FOR OLDER READERS
- *Aliens Are Coming: The True Account of the 1938 "War of the Worlds" Broadcast* by Meghan McCarthy
- *Satchel Paige: Striking Out Jim Crow* by James Sturm
- *Amelia's Itchy-Twitchy, Lovey-Dovey Summer at Camp Mosquito* by Marissa Moss
- *Basketball Bats* by Betty Hicks
- *The Invention of Hugo Cabret* by Brian Selznick
- *Beowulf: A Hero's Tale Retold* by James Rumford
- *Chess Rumble* by Greg Neri
- *The Curse of the Bologna Sandwich (Melvin Beederman, Superhero)* by Greg Trine

Middle-Grade Books

Middle-grade books mark an important milestone in reading development. While picture books, early readers, and chapter books are also significant, they are normally selected for children by adults and often require some dependence on an adult for understanding. Middle-grade books, however, are for the independent reader.

During this phase, children are coming into their own. They are discovering preferences and interests. They are taking up hobbies and making decisions for themselves. They are becoming more aware of the world and their standing in it. Trends, friends, gender, and personal taste influence their reading selections as much as adults do.

FACT

Series are popular with middle-grade readers. Their newfound sense of independence creates a hunger for books. If a child likes one book in a series, chances are he will be pleased with the rest. A series creates a hefty supply of books that a child can rely on, satisfying that hunger with little time needed to find the next good book.

The Design

Middle-grade novels are divided into chapters that are longer than those in chapter books, but not quite as long as those in young adult books. The text is not quite as dense as that of adult novels, but there isn't a whole lot of white space, either. There may be a few illustrations here and there, but not normally more than one per chapter. Middle-grade books usually run between 80 and 192 pages. Word counts vary between 12,000 and 30,000 words.

Writing a Middle-Grade Book

The story line of a middle-grade novel is normally conflict driven. The plot should be clearly defined, and the main character should be someone a child can relate to. It is best to try to keep adult characters to a minimum. While including adults will be necessary in some instances, let the main character (a child) solve the problem or handle the conflict. If an adult steps in to save the day, the child loses her sense of independence.

The main character is important in middle-grade books and should be well-developed.

Middle-grade readers can handle detail as long as you don't drown them in it. At this age they want to be able to create a visual in their minds of the characters and setting. Be as specific as possible and work in the detail naturally. Don't write out detail in a list-like manner; weave it into the story line so that it doesn't stand in the spotlight. Also, try to stay away from describing everything and everyone in the first chapter. Some writers suggest starting your book as late in the story as possible. Think about how you will get the story *moving*, even from the first line. You have plenty of time for the reader to get to know your cast of characters and become familiar with the setting. Present the main character pursuing a goal and facing an obstacle.

EXAMPLES OF MIDDLE-GRADE BOOKS
- *Little House on the Prairie* by Laura Ingalls Wilder
- *A Wrinkle in Time* by Madeleine L'Engle
- *The Indian in the Cupboard* by Lynne Reid Banks
- *Black Beauty* by Anna Sewell
- *Deliver Us from Evie* by M. E. Kerr

Young Adult Books

The young adult (YA) category dangles at the edge of the realm of children's books. Because these books are written for a teenage audience (age twelve and older), they aren't quite children's books per se, yet they aren't adult books either. YA books fall within the children's book category because they are normally published by the children's department of a publishing company or a publishing company that specializes in children's books.

YA books are relatively new. Before the 1960s, the young adult novel was a book published for adults but suitable for teenagers. Now we have books published specifically for teens with teen issues, teen characters, and teen interests, exploring the chaotic world between childhood and adulthood.

Writing YA Books

The teen years are times of trial, pressure, questions, ups and downs, self-consciousness, and drama. As an adult writing for teens, you must try to recapture that tumultuous time. Even though teens may be dealing with adult issues, their priorities and outlooks differ from an adult's. As if teenagers don't have enough to worry about with adult issues, they have their own issues as well. You are free to explore almost any topic in YA books, but if you want to get published, make sure it is in good taste.

FACT

Finding YA books in libraries or bookstores may be a challenging task. Sometimes there is a special section devoted to YA books, but often you will find them shelved with the adult books. Even though they fall into the children's book category, they aren't likely to be found in the children's book section. Teenagers are self-conscious enough as it is. They certainly would not want to be seen looking for books alongside six-year-olds.

Try to remember how you felt as a teenager. What was the most important thing to you at that time? What motivated you? What did you worry about? What tough decisions did you have to make? What kind of pressures did you have to deal with? What were your friends like? Remembering your own teenage years will help you to relate to the teens of today, but keep in mind that times can change rather quickly. You need to stay abreast of today's trends and issues.

Writing for teenagers may give you more of a sense of freedom than writing for younger children. The story should be challenging and thought-provoking. The average teen has a strong vocabulary and can handle complex sentence structures. And because YA books are longer than other children's books, you have more room in which to tell your story. In fact, there is often no difference at all between YA and adult, aside from the age and the concerns of the protagonist.

The examples that follow are books that are so well-written that they appeal to readers of all ages.

EXAMPLES OF YOUNG ADULT BOOKS

- Anne of Green Gables series by Lucy Maud Montgomery
- *To Kill a Mockingbird* by Harper Lee
- *The Catcher in the Rye* by J. D. Salinger
- *The Outsiders* by S. E. Hinton
- *Animal Farm* by George Orwell
- *The Hobbit* by J. R. R. Tolkien
- *Of Mice and Men* by John Steinbeck

CHAPTER 3

Do You Have What It Takes?

Though you may have toyed with the idea of becoming a children's book author and possibly have a few stories already, if you are serious about wanting to break into the field, you need to first determine your motives and goals. This chapter will help you determine whether you have what it takes to become a children's writer.

Your Motives

Children's books may seem easier to write than adult books, but they are not. A lot of hard work, time, and thought goes into each and every one. So what motivates writers to dedicate themselves and put so much effort into a book? Everyone has his own reasons. What are yours?

If you want to contribute to the world of children's literature, you first need to figure out why. Your reasons and sources of motivation will affect your writing, even if only in the smallest way. You need to be aware of this before you can take an objective look at your work.

Fame and Fortune

If you think writing children's books is a quick way to travel down the road to fame and fortune, think again. Though the media may glamorize the life of an author with whirlwind book tours, fancy houses, and limousine service, this isn't typical. Go to a library or bookstore and take a look around. How many books do you see? Now how many authors do you hear about in the media? The numbers don't equate. Many people are published, but few make a complete living from their work.

This isn't to say that you won't be one of the lucky few who do reach fame and fortune; it just means that you shouldn't let this be your driving force. If money provides an incentive to get to work, that's fine. But you should probably have other motivations spurring you on as well if you hope to be happy writing for children.

Writing solely to gain fame and fortune will affect what you write. You will most likely be influenced by the media and the trends it pushes. If you are able to catch a trend and ride it with your work, you might make a pretty penny. However, catching a trend in the publishing industry is a difficult thing to do. Books take several months to years to reach the shelves from the original idea. As you well know, trends are often short-lived and pass by quickly. What was hot yesterday could be lame today.

Passion and Self-Expression

Some people write because they have to. It is more than a hobby; it is a way of life. They find satisfaction in sitting down every day with pen and paper, or at the computer, simply to express themselves. Writing can be very therapeutic and a lot of fun.

Those who are driven by passion and self-expression are very close to their work. If you fall into this category, you should be aware that while loving your work is a good thing, you might sometimes find it difficult to accept criticism. Criticism will be a part of your publishing experience and you will have to learn to accept criticism of your work and not take it as a personal insult.

Sending your work to literary agents or editors is like sending "your baby" off to kindergarten. Agents and editors may be critical or view your work in a different light. They may have suggestions for improvement or flat-out reject it. While this can be discouraging, you should learn from it and move on. Try to take a step back and look at your work objectively. Don't give up!

To Teach or Communicate

Some people set out to become authors of children's books because they want to communicate with a wide audience of children. They feel they have something important to say or teach, and they want to influence and inspire. This is an admirable reason to write children's books, but like the other motives we've just mentioned, it can affect the quality, style, and strength of your work.

ALERT

If you want to reach children with a message, don't preach to them. They will spot a stand-in parent within the very first line and simply disregard the book. Weave your message into a story line and make it entertaining.

When you feel very strongly about a message you want to convey, sometimes your fervor can stand in the way of your storytelling technique and abilities. Perhaps you become so caught up in the importance of the message that you fail to make the book entertaining. Or maybe you write an entertaining story but are so worried that the kids won't get the message that you reiterate constantly. Sometimes the story may be left out altogether and the issue at hand engulfs your writing.

This isn't to say that you should sugarcoat issues. Children are aware of the problems in today's world. If you want to communicate an issue or message to a child, have the characters in your story explore the issue. Allow the characters to suffer consequences of their actions, but also allow the characters to figure out and solve the problem. Try to write a story in which you never state your message outright. Convey the message through dramatization, humor, exaggeration, or point of view.

Self-Discipline

Writing for children takes a lot of hard work and determination. Whether your goal is to build a writing career or simply to publish one book, it all begins with self-discipline. Writing is a strange activity, because it is both work and play. While you certainly may derive great amounts of pleasure from writing, it's not playtime. You have to set goals, be strict with yourself, and resist the temptation to put it aside when you're frustrated.

Making Time

You must learn how to relax and allow subconscious thoughts and feelings to emerge. Yet you must keep to a schedule, and not simply wait around for inspiration. How can you have it both ways? There are only two ways to write: either on a strict schedule or when inspiration strikes. Each method offers an important path to creative accomplishment.

It is almost impossible to find time to write during the day. Meetings run long, the kids need to be picked up and dropped off, unexpected crises catch us off guard, and the housework is always waiting to be done. How are you supposed to find the time to sit down and write? You won't; you need to make the time and put yourself on a strict schedule.

You must take your writing seriously and elevate it to a level of importance. Don't consider it a leisure activity; make it a part of your day—every day. If you use some type of daily planner, pencil in an allotted time to write. If you live day by day without a schedule, consider getting up earlier or going to bed later and use that extra time to write.

When are you most productive? Are you a morning person or a night owl? Use part of your most productive time to write, even if it's only an hour while the baby sleeps. Some highly accomplished and successful writers of children's books started that way. Making time for your writing may seem even more daunting than the writing itself, but you must do it. It is better to have a short writing period when you are at your best than a long one when you are tired or distracted.

Once you have established a specific time to write and stick to it every day, you will be surprised how much more productive you will become. Your brain gets used to that time when it is "supposed" to open channels to your imagination. It "knows" you won't be interrupted, and it will begin to drop its normal anxiety about handling your busy life.

ESSENTIAL

If your life seems harried and unorganized and you don't believe it is possible to set aside writing time every day, you may want to consider making use of a time management system. There are several books and courses that will help you to take control of your time and increase the quality of life.

Even if you prefer to write on a strict schedule, sometimes a great idea will come to you at an inconvenient time. You might be falling asleep after a long hard day, for instance. If you want to reap the benefits of this gift from your subconscious to your conscious mind, you must get up and write it down! Keep your notebook and pen available at all times. It might not take long to jot down an idea, or you might be swept into your story and write for hours.

Learn to use both methods, because the strict schedule method is necessary for finishing projects and managing a career, and the "inspiration strikes" method will reveal your most creative thoughts. The first method requires steady determination; its virtue is patience. The second method requires alertness to your imagination; its virtue is self-trust.

Setting Goals

Your ultimate goal is to write a good book. Always keep that in focus. An important secondary goal is to get published. To accomplish both goals, break them down into smaller goals or milestones. Your sense of accomplishment in reaching each of the smaller goals will help motivate you through the next one. For instance, important goals in the early stages of writing include research, writing character biographies, and experimenting with storytelling viewpoints. Another goal may be to create an outline for your story. Some writers work best from brief outlines; others thrive only on elaborate ones.

Be realistic when setting your goals. Set a deadline for yourself and work solely on just one of these steps. Don't push yourself too hard, and remember that goals are not set in stone. You may find that you need more time with a particular goal. Sometimes a writer just needs to sit and stare, daydream, and let an image or line of dialogue float into consciousness. Only by focusing on baby steps, one at a time, will you discover the writing process that works best for you.

FACT

Think of your imagination as a creative child locked in a room. When she looks out the window she sees you managing your day—planning meals, caring for others, driving a car, or becoming distracted by radio or television. She waits for the Strict Schedule Method and the Inspiration Strikes Methods to unlock the door and let her outside to play.

Rewarding Yourself

While you should definitely take your writing seriously and work hard, this doesn't mean that there isn't room for a little fun. You should reward yourself for accomplishments. Set up a reward system that complements the tasks completed. For instance, when you complete an initial draft outline of your book, treat yourself: go out for an ice cream, take a walk or a bike ride on a beautiful day, or watch a favorite movie.

Tools of the Trade

In theory, all you really need to have to write a children's story is a pen and a piece of paper—and in fact, this is all you need to get started. But these days, a computer has become the one truly necessary piece of equipment for a writer—at least for a writer with hopes of getting published. Editors require either printed or e-mailed manuscripts, so regardless of your preferences during the writing process, you will eventually have to type your work.

Computer Savvy?

While you may wish to compose first drafts using pen and notebook, typing your story into a computer's word processing program makes revision much easier. When your draft appears on the screen it becomes easier to visualize as a book, and you can enter changes quickly. If you haven't already done this, invest a little time each day learning to type properly. Once your fingers have the feel of the keys, ideas fly quickly from your mind to the page. Many writers find this less tiring than working with a pen. If typing is not your thing, one of the newer technologies you may wish to try is voice-recognition software. If you record a story digitally, using the microphone in your computer or an external mic, there are software programs that can instantly translate your audio into written text.

Of course, while you might be comfortable making up stories for kids, and you might enjoy oral storytelling, when you're all alone in a room you might find it difficult to talk to a computer. Like learning to tell stories aloud, and learning to write stories with a pen or a keyboard, learning to compose while speaking into a recording device takes a little practice. But think of the advantages. You are out for a walk, and you see squirrels chasing each other; then you notice blue jays chasing each other, and the next thing you know, bunnies are chasing each other. You pull out your little digital recorder with its built-in mic, and start talking: "Story idea. *Animals chasing animals*. Squirrels chase each other like streaks of gray in the leaves, over the grass and the moss, up in trees and out in the breeze. Blue jays are raucous and squawkous; they are streaks of blue in the sky. Bunnies dash around without sound; they chase each other in circles on the ground."

When you get home, plug your recorder into your computer, just as you would download pictures from your camera, and transfer your story notes to your word processing program. Later you can view the text, push a key and cast it into a favorite font such as Courier, and add more lines. Soon you have the draft of a picture book that you'd never have captured without that little digital recorder. As you become used to working this way, you may be able to dictate much longer stories.

Practical Tips

Along with the computer, you will need a printer. While it is fairly common to e-mail manuscripts to editors, some editors work entirely on hard copy. You will also need a printer for cover letters and other correspondence. Save your work in two places: on the hard drive of your computer and on an external drive. This can be an expensive unit capable of storing copies of everything on your hard drive, or an inexpensive USB flash drive that weighs about one ounce, stores up to 250 GB, and can be carried in your pocket.

Internet access provides a wonderful helping hand to writers. You will use it to research the market, publishing companies, and background for your story. The Internet has a wealth of information readily available. Plus, it offers websites, message boards, and social media groups dedicated to children's writing, which may be able to answer some of your questions and help you with the writing process.

ALERT

Don't rely solely on the Internet for all of your research needs. Anyone can create a website, and not every site offers accurate information. Double check your sources if you choose to use the Internet for research information.

If you are lucky enough to sell your book to a publisher, you will probably communicate with your editor via e-mail. Editors find that e-mail is less time-consuming than telephone calls or letters. Remember to keep copies of all of your correspondence, including e-mail. Back up your files frequently so that you have a record of all communications.

Writer's References

There are several reference books you will need to have on hand to take you through the writing process. If you want to present a clean manuscript to an editor, these books will certainly come in handy. Building your own library will save you time and energy, as you will probably refer to these books often.

First of all, you need a comprehensive and up-to-date dictionary. The pocket dictionaries will not do. There is a certain comfort in seeing a large, hardbound, complete dictionary and knowing that thousands of words are available to you. If you use the dictionary in your word processing program or a free one on the Internet, be sure to check more than one source.

Almost hand in hand with a dictionary is a thesaurus. It is satisfying to own a comprehensive hardbound edition, but you will find good ones in your software and free ones online.

The *Chicago Manual of Style* is used by many publishing houses. Visit the website of the University of Chicago Press for an extensive list of resource books for writers. A great little book to refer to for style and grammar is Strunk and White's *Elements of Style.* If you have ever taken a writing class, you probably already own this. It is a concise book that reviews the rules of style, punctuation, and grammar.

You will find many helpful sources by typing words like "copyright," "children's publishers," "grammar," and "writer's resources" into a search engine. Feel free to make use of Wikipedia, but bear in mind that it is publicly created. It's great for an introduction to a subject, but double check information that is crucial to your project.

Dedicated Space

Not only will you need to dedicate time to writing, but you will also need to dedicate space. If you want to do your best work, you will need to concentrate solely on your writing, at least for specified periods of time. This is best accomplished by dedicating a particular area of your home to a workstation. Looking around you, you may think that this is next to impossible. Well, it just may be time to do a little rearranging.

If you have a spare room or study, the task will be an easy one. However, if you don't have that extra rarely used space, you will have to get creative. Maybe you have an attic or basement that could be turned into a small home office. If not, take a good look at the space available in the other rooms of your home. Do your children have a playroom? Perhaps you could work in there while the children are at school or after they have gone to bed.

Look for the least used areas of the house. Setting up a workstation in the living room may not be such a great idea if the rest of your family spends most of their time there. (You also wouldn't want the added distraction or temptation of the television.) Do you have a dining room that is used only in the evenings? Or maybe you could rearrange your bedroom furniture and designate a corner of the room as your workstation.

Once you have chosen an area, you need to organize it to make the best use of the space. At the very least, you will need a desk and good lighting. You may also want to make room for a filing cabinet and bookcase. You will want all of your reference materials within reach so you don't waste time and concentration getting up and walking across the room for needed materials.

ALERT

If you choose to use an attic or basement as your dedicated writing space, make sure you have plenty of good light. Often these two places don't get as much natural light as does the rest of the house. Poor lighting will create eyestrain and headaches.

If your family is home during your scheduled writing time, talk to them and stress how important it is that you are not disturbed when you are at your workstation. But don't expect too much. Families never leave writers in peace for very long, so be careful not to blame them for interrupting you. Your goal, however, should be a time and place of true solitude—as soon as you can manage it. Whether you write behind a closed door, or after everyone goes to sleep, or before they wake up, it is up to you to make it happen.

A Realistic Outlook

If you are serious about writing children's books, it helps to know what you are getting into. At the risk of sounding discouraging, the world of children's publishing is not for everyone. You must be patient, persistent, hardworking, and certainly have a bit of talent. There are talented authors out there who haven't been published though they have done their homework and know the market inside and out.

Children's publishers receive thousands of manuscripts a year and only a small percentage of those make it to print. To be able to compete with and stand out from these thousands of other writers, you have to write, revise, and send out your work. Put these three words on a note card above your desk: "Write, revise, send." They are the three essential activities, and you must develop a schedule, a place, and the discipline to execute them every week.

Don't Quit Your Day Job

Children's publishing is not the way to an overnight fortune. Even if you believe in your ability to write successfully, now is not the time to quit your current job. You will need the money to survive while you struggle through the obstacles every writer faces.

It often takes writers several years and several published books before they are able to become full-time writers. As a writer you won't receive a steady income that you can predict and rely upon. Writing is hard enough. If you add the stress and pressure of relying on a book to be a moneymaker, your work will be affected and you won't be able to give 100 percent to it.

FACT

If you work as a full-time writer, decide on how many hours a day you will work and stick to it. Treat your writing as you would any other job and respect work time as well as personal time. If you haven't mastered the art of self-discipline, it can be easy to fall behind in your work.

A Lonely Life

Let's say that after years of blood, sweat, and tears, you achieve your goal: You are a full-time writer. Certainly you should be thrilled about your success and celebrate appropriately, but after all the party guests have gone, you might find yourself sitting down to a very lonely occupation.

If you made time to write while maintaining a full-time job, you know that peace and quiet are moments to be treasured and taken advantage of. However, if you quit your job to become a full-time writer, you may find that the peace and quiet you once treasured soon becomes an annoyance.

Especially if you have just come from a busy office environment, the silence, broken only by the hum of your computer, can be quite distracting. The lack of human interaction may take its toll on you and affect your work. You may find yourself wanting to do the laundry, wash the dishes, or even watch talk shows on television—anything other than sitting in the quiet staring at a blank screen.

Writing is something you have to do on your own; there's really no getting around it. You have to be someone who can concentrate while spending several hours alone. Does this sound like you? You need to take this into consideration before taking the plunge into full-time writing. Knowing what to expect may help to make that transition a little easier.

Words of Encouragement

So you've made it through a reality check without backing out. Good. Don't give up. Writing for children is a rewarding experience on many levels. Keep focused on your pleasure in writing, the fun of researching a topic that moves you, and the joy in finishing a story. Cultivate and learn to enjoy the revision process. Take the tasks of researching agents and publishers as a challenge, and meet it with spirit.

There are thousands of writers on the same path as you. But you may not realize that only a small percentage of these writers conduct the proper research to find a publisher that fits their book. Only a few do the needed market research. Only a few follow the individual submission guidelines of the publishers. Only a few write and rewrite constantly until they get it just right.

Thousands of children's books are published each year, which means that thousands of writers are needed each year. If you play by the rules and learn all you can about children's publishing, you stand a chance at success.

Most important of all, remember that your well-written story is a source of pride. It's an accomplishment that is hard to beat, regardless of how it fares in the marketplace.

CHAPTER 4

Furthering Your Education

There are several venues open to writers to help them strengthen their skills, get answers to their questions, and learn more about the craft. Whether you are a beginning writer or a seasoned author, you will benefit from taking advantage of one or several of the options explored in this chapter.

Opening Yourself to Criticism

Before you sign up for any course, workshop, or writers' group, you need to first accept that your work is going to be criticized. This isn't to say that people are going to shout out how awful it is, but it does mean that people will assess your work and its imperfections.

Learning to accept criticism is not an easy thing to do. Your work is a part of you, and it is easy to regard criticism as a personal insult. But your close relationship with your work can hinder you from looking at it objectively. That's where criticism steps in. Once you finally decide to release your work from the shelter of your safekeeping, it is open to interpretation. Getting the objective opinion of several people before sending your work off to a publishing company will help to make your work the best it can be. It will also prepare you for the criticism that you will most likely face from an editor.

Outside the Family

While it is always good for the ego to get the opinion of family and friends, unless they are willing to be honest with you, their opinions are probably going to be biased. They might exclaim that it is the best story they have ever read or shower you with other such praise. This of course is always pleasant to hear, but it really isn't going to help you better your work. If you truly want constructive criticism, show your work to people who don't know you, or at least don't know you very well. They will be more likely to give you an honest opinion. Writers' groups, classes, and workshops are good places to learn from criticism. In these forums, people work together, providing valuable feedback and support. The advantage of these settings is that feedback is generally monitored and controlled by a moderator or group leader, so you needn't ever feel as though you are being attacked. Remember that group members are there first to help themselves, and second to help you. Keep that in mind and open yourself to the ideas of others. Remember to be kind when you give your honest appraisal of the work of your fellow group members or classmates.

It's All Yours

As you actively seek constructive criticism of your work, you will soon learn whose opinions are well-thought-out and supported and whose are watered down and vague. Use your judgment. You needn't feel as though you should make every change that others suggest. With this in mind, you will find criticism helpful, and may even come to welcome it.

ALERT

Get used to criticism before submitting your work to an editor or agent.

Since these people hold the key to your dreams, you may be quite sensitive to their criticism. However, if you have learned to take criticism in stride, you can use their feedback to improve your work.

Of course, the story is always your own and you have the final authority. You can either take or leave the suggestions of others. But if you truly want to make your work the best it can be, you will at least consider any advice given.

Writers' Groups

A writers' group is an excellent forum for feedback and sharing information. Here you will meet other writers who are facing the same challenges you are. It is always comforting to know that you aren't the only one out there struggling to make your dreams come true.

Several communities have writers' groups already established. In your local area, check with libraries, schools, and community bulletin boards for information. If you come up empty-handed, start your own group!

Writers' groups don't have one set agenda. Some gather solely to critique one another's works. Some are open to anything concerning the publishing industry, such as discussions about market trends, contracts, editors, and reviews. Some will bring in guest speakers from time to time, such as a published author or editor. Some simply combine all these elements and go with the flow. Whatever type of group you choose to join (or start), you will find it a rather casual and comfortable atmosphere in which to further your knowledge of the writing process.

Benefits of a Writers' Group

As an aspiring author, you will benefit tremendously by joining a writers' group. Not only will you learn from shared information, but you will also find the support that you might not otherwise receive. If you work in a busy office, you may constantly have the support of your colleagues, even if the support is only in the form of their physical presence. Writing, on the other hand, often leaves you with a feeling of isolation and lack of support. Since writing can be a very lonely occupation, it helps to get out of the house and meet with others who are traveling a similar path. Getting comfortable talking about writing will also help develop your critical reading skills, which will in turn aid in improving your work.

Once enmeshed in your writers' group, take advantage of the shared information and listen to speakers carefully. Your group is likely to be made up of people from a variety of professions and personal backgrounds, which means the scope of information available will have a wide range. Perhaps one member is a former editor and can give you insider information on the publishing industry. Another may be the mother of three children who can give you advice on how to make your child characters more realistic. Be an active and supportive member of your group, and you may both improve your writing and score some invaluable contacts.

ESSENTIAL

Don't forget that you need to give gently as well as take. Don't sit silently in the corner until you are called upon to read your work. Share your opinions and ideas, even if you believe your contribution won't be earth-shattering.

Making Friends

You will probably become good friends with other members of the group. Though it sounds counterintuitive, this may actually put a dent in the usefulness of the group. Friends may be hesitant to tell you anything negative. During a critique of your work, you may find that your newfound friends only praise you. This is nice to hear, but defeats the purpose of the group. Another hazard is that a disagreement between friends can trigger an unnecessarily harsh critique that may damage the self-esteem of the aspiring author.

ESSENTIAL

Don't be afraid to ask questions of the members of a writers' group. Everyone has different levels of experience in the writing process. Never feel as though your question is stupid; it is quite likely that another member of the group needs it answered as well.

If you feel that friendship is affecting the usefulness of the group, say something. Let it be known that you are open to and welcome constructive criticism. If there is a tiff affecting the critique, try to get it solved or at least reach an agreement that it will not carry over into the group.

Consider a Class

Perhaps you have fantastic ideas for children's books, but when you sit down to actually write them, you find that your writing skills aren't so fantastic. Don't take this as an omen telling you to stop writing. Instead, congratulate yourself for recognizing a weakness and do something about it!

FACT

Sometimes professors will allow you to sit in on a couple of their classes before you actually decide to sign up. If you are unsure whether a class is appropriate for you, contact the professor or admissions office and see if this option is available.

Visit local colleges and universities and pick up a copy of their course listings (you may want to check out the adult education or continuing education departments for these). Browse through and highlight classes that could help you strengthen your skills.

Before you rush to sign up for a full course load, consider the time you have available to devote to a class. Make sure you take into consideration the time it will take to commute to and from the school. Keep in mind that to get your money's worth out of a class, you have to actually learn something. This means attending every class you possibly can, devoting your attention to the instructor during class time, and, of course, doing your homework. Taking a class is a big responsibility. Make sure you can dedicate the time and energy before signing up.

Degree Programs

After considering your options, you may decide that you want to go beyond a single course or writers' group. You may want to consider a full degree program. In recent years, the scholarly study of children's writing and literature has widened, and now the options for continuing your education in writing for children and young adults are numerous. The Children's Literature Association lists more than twenty-five colleges and universities offering degree programs in the field of children's literature. There are also a handful of schools offering Master of Fine Arts (MFA) degrees in writing for children. This list is not comprehensive, but merely a place to begin your research.

- The New School, offering a traditional residency MFA program
- Hollins University, offering both an MA and MFA, both brief-residency
- Spalding University, offering a brief-residency MFA program
- Vermont College, offering a brief-residency MFA program
- Hamline University, offering a brief-residency MFA program
- Simmons College, offering a traditional residency MFA as well as a dual degree in Children's Literature and Writing for Children, MA/MFA
- Whidbey Island Writers Association, offering a brief-residency MFA program run by a writers' association, not a college or university

FACT

The Institute of Children's Literature offers a quality course in children's writing. Visit its website at *www.institutechildrenslit.com* to take a free aptitude test, view a sample lesson, and receive additional information.

Other writing programs offer courses in writing for children as part of a broader creative writing curriculum. However, MFA programs are on the rise, and in the next few years, you can expect to see a number of additional writing for children and young adult degree program options.

For help finding the degree program for you, check the Children's Literature Association website (*www.childlitassn.org*), Poets and Writers Magazine (*www.pw.org*), and the Association of Writers and Writing Programs (*www.awpwriter.org*) for updated listings.

Writers' Organizations

There are several writers' organizations that provide information on the ins and outs of writing and publishing, and some are specific to children's books. This is a very competitive field, and the more information you can arm yourself with, the easier it will be to set yourself apart from other writers. The catch is that some writers' organizations require you to be published before you can join. But even those that do require publishing history may offer information and activities to nonmembers (for a fee, of course).

The following sections highlight a few, but there are others out there, so don't limit yourself to just these.

FACT

Writers' conferences are great places to meet valuable contacts, and sometimes for an extra fee an agent or editor will read a short manuscript. Never force your manuscript on anyone you meet here. Exude professionalism and politeness and you may just meet a helpful contact.

Society of Children's Book Writers and Illustrators

The Society of Children's Book Writers and Illustrators (SCBWI) is an international organization devoted to children's literature. It offers extensive information on all areas of children's publishing and publishes the bimonthly *Bulletin,* which provides up-to-date market information. Members also receive free literature on topics such as contracts, copyright information, author's rights, and agents. The organization offers lists of publishers. The SCBWI sponsors writers' conferences, and members receive discounts for these conferences. Members report that SCBWI events are very helpful.

The SCBWI is an invaluable source of information, and if you are serious about becoming an author of children's books, it is recommended that you join. Membership is open to both published and unpublished writers and illustrators. For more information about SCBWI, visit its website at *www.scbwi.org*; write to SCBWI, 8271 Beverly Boulevard, Los Angeles, CA 90048; or call 323-782-1010.

The Authors Guild

The Authors Guild is a professional organization devoted to advocating the rights of writers. Membership is open only to those who have been published by an American publisher. It offers useful information and tips for writers interested in protecting their rights by addressing issues such as contract negotiation and electronic publishing.

It publishes *The Authors Guild Bulletin*, which features articles covering issues specific to authors as well as current news (and gossip) about the publishing industry. You will also find a section devoted to personnel changes in the publishing industry, such as who has left what company and title changes.

For more information about the Authors Guild, visit its website at *www.authorsguild.org*; write to The Authors Guild, 31 East 28th Street, 10th Floor, New York, NY 10016; or call 212-563-5904.

The Children's Book Council

The Children's Book Council is a nonprofit organization dedicated to children's literature. Its members consist of publishers and packagers of trade children's books in the United States. While individual writers are not allowed membership, you can access its publications, some free of charge, some requiring a small fee. Many writers find the Council's publications to be very informative and a good source for market and publishing company research.

The Children's Book Council publishes a list of its members. This list includes a general description of the company, its address and telephone number, and submission guidelines. The list includes the names of personnel to contact. The Children's Book Council also publishes information specific to writers and illustrators about the children's publishing world and offers tips on how to best present your material.

For more information about the Children's Book Council, visit its website at *www.cbcbooks.org*; write to The Children's Book Council, 12 West 37th Street, 2nd Floor, New York, NY 10018; or call 212-966-1990.

Seminars and Workshops

Writers often find participating in workshops and seminars to be great learning experiences. The advantage of formal seminars and workshops over writers' groups is that you will most likely meet different people each time you attend. Therefore, you will be getting more critiques, more information, and more contacts. However, while writers' groups are often free, you will almost always pay a fee for attending a seminar or workshop. If money is a little tight, go as far as you can with free critiques and information-sharing before paying to rub elbows with strangers.

Getting Your Money's Worth from Seminars

Seminars are often conducted in a manner similar to classes. Normally the main attraction is the speaker. Seminars featuring best-selling authors and top editors are often advertised nationwide. Therefore, if you attend one of these seminars, chances are you will have the opportunity to meet and make friends with people from all over the country. The more widespread your friends, the more widespread your contacts—and it always helps to have friends in the industry.

There are also more localized seminars that feature experienced authors or editors, but depending on where you live, perhaps not as well-known. However, these are no less educational than the others, so don't snub them. You probably won't have to pay as much for these as you would for the nationally advertised seminars.

Seminars are often advertised in trade publications and through writers' organizations, as well as online. If you are interested in attending a seminar, make sure it covers a topic of interest to you before signing up.

Workshops Can Work for You

Workshops run from one afternoon to several weeks long, to accommodate the spectrum of attendees. Sometimes these events are even tied into a vacation activity, such as skiing, or take place at fancy spa resorts or rustic farms. The activities are often very similar to those of writers' groups. While the agenda varies, you will almost always have an opportunity to discuss your writing with a group (to "workshop" your work). You may also have an opportunity to work one-on-one with a professional in the industry.

If you are interested in attending a writers' workshop, search the Internet, look through trade publications, and ask around. But make sure you know what you are getting into. Who will be conducting the workshop—is it an experienced author or editor? How much does the workshop cost? What is included in the cost? What is on the agenda? How much personal attention will you receive? While you will certainly gain *some* knowledge from any workshop, try to get the most for your money.

ESSENTIAL

Because you will be paying an admission fee, you probably should have a finished (or at least close to finished) manuscript to take along with you before attending a workshop. You don't want to walk in there with just a bunch of jumbled ideas.

Working One-on-One

At any stage in your writing journey, you may wish to work one-on-one with an experienced author or editor. The detailed feedback you receive working individually can build your confidence as a writer as much as it can strengthen your abilities.

If you want to strengthen your general writing abilities and brush up on grammar, punctuation, spelling, and structure, an author or editor could help you, regardless of whether or not he is involved in children's publishing. However, if you want to learn the specifics of children's writing, you should probably look for someone who specializes in that field.

Many professional editors, writers, and writing teachers offer one-on-one manuscript consultation services. These services vary depending on the needs of the client; one emerging writer may want to hire someone to copy-edit her work before she queries it for publication, while another may want support during the early writing process—this person may seek more a writing "mentor" or "coach." There may be mentors living in your area available to discuss the work in person, while others from around the country will work over mail, e-mail, and the phone.

These are all great options, but before handing over your money, be sure to do a little background research. Remember that anyone can set up a website, and don't rely solely on one source of background information (especially not personal web pages). What books has this person worked on? What is the quality of these books? How long has this person worked in the children's publishing industry?

If you are satisfied with the results of your research, you can proceed to contact this person. Send a brief letter that states where you got his name and what type of instruction you are interested in, and inquire whether he has the time and desire to meet with you, or to see your work. Keep the letter simple and polite. Include your contact information and times when you can be reached. Fees will vary with the type and amount of work to be done. Some professionals have a set hourly rate, while others determine their fees on a per-project basis. Be sure to verify the fee structure before sending your work.

ESSENTIAL

If you have trouble locating a suitable writer or editor to work with, check local colleges and universities. Editors sometimes advertise their services through university bulletins, and teachers in writing and English departments may offer one-on-one services on the side.

With luck, you will receive a positive response. If you do, set up a meeting in which you will discuss the specifics of the tutoring session(s)—time, place, fee, and so on. During this initial meeting, make sure you are very specific about what it is you hope to accomplish. If you are a good writer but need help with character development, say so. If you are just getting started following your dreams of writing books for children, tell him that. The more this individual knows, the more he can help.

CHAPTER 5

Researching the Market

There's no getting around it: You need to arm yourself with knowledge of the marketplace. It is important for a writer to be aware of what is happening in the world of children's publishing, not only to maintain an edge that many other writers don't have but also to discover the best way of reaching the intended audience.

Knowledge Is Power

Knowledge is power. Ignorance is bliss. As a writer, you want the power. It is unlikely that you would give a speech on cold fusion in front of thousands of people if you had no knowledge of the subject. Nor would you walk into a job interview without the slightest idea of what the company does. Well, neither should you try to convince a publisher that your manuscript should be turned into a book without the knowledge of what is currently selling. The more knowledge you have of the market, the better chance you stand of getting the attention of an editor.

Welcome to the Business

You must keep in mind that publishing is a business, and the success of publishing companies relies on their ability to sell books. So although publishers do seek to bring great literature to the world, they must focus on sales in order to stay afloat. As a writer aspiring to get published, you can't ignore the business aspect.

Unfortunately, most editors will first look at the salability of a book and then look at its quality. If you want your manuscript to make a good first impression, your best bet is to show your knowledge of the marketplace and how your book will thrive within it. You won't be able to write a convincing query or cover letter without the power of that knowledge behind you.

What to Watch

There are several things you will need to keep an eye out for. Pay attention to what is selling well. Read reviews of new children's books and interviews with both up-and-coming and seasoned authors. Talk to your local librarians and booksellers and find out which books children and parents are asking for. What subjects are most popular for different age groups? What topics have been beaten to death? Find out the differences in what girls and boys read. Notice the physical appearance of the books. Are hard covers or paperbacks more prominent? What are popular trim sizes and page counts? The questions are endless, but these will get you started.

Watch the news, listen to the radio, and see what catches your attention. Maybe an idea for a children's book will come from the evening weather

report or from your favorite baseball team. You never know when inspiration will strike, so keep your senses alert.

ESSENTIAL

While you may find researching the market and children's publishing overwhelming now, once you know where to look and become accustomed to pricking up your ears at key words and phrases, the ongoing research will become second nature. Just keep in mind that every little tidbit of information you can store in your mind about children's publishing is useful.

Aside from the books themselves, keep track of the publishing companies. Mergers and acquisitions happen all the time, so stay up-to-date on which companies have joined and what type of books each publishing company produces. Some publishing companies produce only children's books, some produce only adult books, and some produce both adult and children's books. And within these broad divisions are subdivisions based on subject matter and type of books published. There is a lot to learn and a lot to keep up with, but you will find the time and energy well spent when you see your book sitting alongside other great children's books on the shelf.

The Big Picture

Before you begin researching the specifics of the children's publishing industry, you should take a look at the big picture. By understanding the various markets available to children's books, you will be able to make choices concerning your own writing and take steps to zero in on specific areas. Keep in mind that the following markets are quite broad and allow room for a wide variety of subject matters and styles.

Trade Market

Trade books are most often defined as books that are sold in bookstores. These books are usually higher-priced, higher-quality books that can be either fiction or nonfiction. While most think of trade books as hardcover books, trade publishers also produce paperbacks. The trade market is what most people think of when they think of bookselling. Unless you want to write for a small, specialized audience or use technical language, you will most likely be writing for the trade market.

Mass Market

Mass-market books are paperbacks that are lower-priced, lower-quality books sold in supermarkets, discount department stores, newsstands, drugstores, and so on. Mass-market books normally have a smaller trim size and are designed to appeal to a different audience from the one that buys trade books.

Mass-market children's books are often tied in to a popular show or character. The publishers often come up with the concept and then search out authors to follow their guidelines. In addition to seeking this market for your own work, you may want to look into working for publishers on established series. It is possible to be hired as a writer for a preconceived line of mass-market titles.

FACT

One of the biggest publishing niches is the religious market. There are some publishers who produce only religious materials to sell to religious bookstores and organizations. Religious books can be fiction or nonfiction, but always convey a message specific to a particular belief.

Institutional Market

The institutional market covers schools and libraries. Someone has to write and publish the textbooks that kids use in school, right? Often textbooks are curriculum-based and developed by the publisher. However, schools are beginning to add more and more single-title books to their curricula. Therefore, you can find publishers who produce high-quality fiction and nonfiction books that can be sold to bookstores, libraries, and schools.

Titles in the institutional market span a wide range of subjects. While there is certainly a need for those books in academic subjects such as science, health, and math, there is also a need for books covering

- *Horn Book* (*www.hbook.com*) is a bimonthly magazine that contains reviews of children's books and features articles on issues pertaining solely to children's literature.

NEWSLETTERS
- *Children's Book Insider* (*www.write4kids.com*) is a monthly newsletter for children's writers offering writing tips, market information, submission tips, advice from authors, and articles covering a variety of topics.
- *Children's Writer* (*www.childrenswriter.com*), published by the Institute of Children's Literature, is a monthly newsletter for children's writers offering market information and articles on the writing craft, publishers, and editors.

WRITERS' MAGAZINES
- *Writer's Digest* (*www.writersdigest.com*) is a magazine for writers that offers articles on agents, contracts, self-publishing; interviews with professionals in the industry; and occasionally news on children's publishing.
- *The Writer* (*www.writermag.com*) is a monthly magazine offering submission tips, market information, and informative articles for all fields of writing.

Children's Magazines

While magazines designed specifically for children will not provide information on the publishing industry's ins and outs, they do provide an insight into children's interests. If you subscribe to a variety of magazines, you will be able to compare repeated topics and how they are handled.

ESSENTIAL

Several authors of children's books found their start publishing stories in children's magazines. This is a great way to get your work out there, and since children's magazines are published more frequently than books, their publishers are usually looking for new authors more often than book publishers are.

If there is a section contributed to by readers, pay particular attention to it. For instance, maybe the magazine allows children to write letters to the editor or showcase their own stories and artwork. Here you will find what children of this age group are interested in.

Networking

Another great way to find out what's happening in the children's publishing world is to talk to people involved in the industry. Maybe you know someone who knows someone who knows someone who could give you an insider's scoop.

If you have joined a writers' group, then you may already have contacts at your fingertips. Ask specific questions of the members. More often than not, these groups welcome the sharing of industry info.

Become a fan of popular children's book writers on Facebook and follow them on Twitter. Their comments might give you some insight into their creative process. Check out websites devoted to children's publishing. Most publishing companies will have a social media presence—sign up for as many groups as you can. Post an inquiry on a message board or sit in on an online discussion. Be friendly and inquisitive, and don't hesitate to offer information that you have gathered as well. Perhaps you will find contact information for the person hosting the site. If he is unable to answer your question, he may be able to recommend someone who can.

Take advantage of all the resources available to you. Keep in mind that everyone has busy schedules, so be as accommodating as you can—your patience may win you brownie points with someone who proves to be an invaluable source of information. Be persistent, but not aggressive.

Finding a Gap in the Market

During your research you may come across topics that are currently unexplored in children's publishing, but desirable to children. If this happens, jump on it. Tapping into unexplored territory can be both exciting and lucrative.

Although it may seem as though every subject has been covered already, we are creating history every day. New technologies emerge, new discoveries are made, new events take place, and new issues are brought to the forefront. If you have a specialty, such as in medicine or horticulture, you are probably aware of current happenings or the latest research in your field. Could any of these advancements be the subject of a children's book?

Finding a gap in the market doesn't always mean that the subject is completely new—just that it is underserved in children's literature. You may find that an existing subject has not yet been explored in the form of a children's book. Or maybe it already has, but the book may be out of print or outdated. Can you give a fresh take on an old book?

If you believe you have discovered a subject that has not already been explored and would make a fantastic children's book, don't rush to contact an editor while shouting that you have her next bestseller. Just because your research hasn't come across a book on that particular topic doesn't mean that one doesn't exist. You certainly don't want to contact an editor and heighten the editor's expectations only to hear her voice—tinged with disappointment and annoyance—telling you that the subject matter has already been tackled and that it bombed in the children's book industry. Do your homework, and when you contact an editor with an idea, do so with a balanced tone.

Directing Your Attention

While it is best to stay up-to-date on all aspects of children's publishing, if you have decided what type of book you would like to write (or if you already have something written) then you will want to zero in on that during your research. For instance, if you are a history buff and are interested in historical fiction picture books, you should research the track records of previously published books in that area.

By Topic

Take a close look at all the books covering your topic and compare them to yours. How is your book different? What does it offer readers that others don't? You will have to convince an editor that yours has an advantage. Therefore, you must know the market for these books. You also need to find out how well these books sell.

Look for updated information or statistics concerning your topic. If you can improve upon or add a new twist to a topic that has already been covered extensively, then you might have a shot at grabbing an editor's attention. On the other hand, if the topic has had little coverage, you need to consider why. Perhaps other writers simply haven't been able to make it exciting. Or it may be that the topic is not one children are naturally drawn to. Editors may have decided that your topic does not work for children's books—in this case, you will have to present them with an undeniably catchy idea.

ESSENTIAL

Look up reviews of books that are similar to yours. This will give you an idea of the expectations for these books. Also take a look at the publication dates. It may be that you can add updated information, giving a stale topic a fresh outlook.

By Type of Book

Perhaps you don't know exactly what topic you want to cover, but you have a sense of what *type* of book you want to write. For instance, maybe you are fascinated with picture books and can't see yourself writing anything but. Or maybe you want to deal only with the facts and prefer writing nonfiction.

Let's say you want to write chapter books. See if bookstores and libraries have a particular section devoted to chapter books. If so, you are in luck. Take an afternoon and don't stray from that section. Pick up every book that catches your eye and flip through it. What topics do chapter books explore? How many pages do they have? How are the covers designed? What are the trim sizes? What sets these books apart from the rest of the children's books at the store?

Try to find out what chapter books are the most popular with children—and with adults. Compare the chapter book section with the picture books, early readers, and middle-grade books. Which section is the largest? Which is the smallest? Ask around to find out what chapter books are the best known to kids and adults, not just booksellers and librarians. Also try to find out what books were disappointing to readers. If you can determine what helps a book to sell and what causes it to fail, you will have a head start on writing a successful chapter book.

Of course, you will also want to pay attention to new releases and interviews with chapter book authors. Read through industry publications and find out what's happening in the world of chapter books. Which publishing companies publish chapter books? Keep an eye on these and how they market their products.

CHAPTER 6

Cultivating the Idea

Before you can begin to write, you must have a feeling for a story—though you may not know much of the story yet. This is the starting point for all writers and must be handled with care. This chapter shows you how to organize what you have, how to capture new characters, images, and ideas, and how to develop your story in the process of writing.

The Notebook, Your Best Friend

It's happened to every writer at one time or another: You are hit unexpectedly by the best idea you've ever had, but when it comes time to make use of that idea, it is forever lost in the crevices of your mind. Invest in a small notebook to carry around with you at all times. You never know when a great idea for a story, a character, or even a character's name, will strike you; if you are prepared, you can jot it down and not have to worry about trying to remember it.

Jot down everything that catches your interest. Don't worry about trying to piece together an entire story from one observation. Just write it down and move on to the next thing that pops into your head or attracts your eye. If you harp on one idea, you might miss out on other, more useful observations and ideas for your children's book.

ALERT

It's a good idea to attach a pen or pencil to your notebook by clipping it or tying it with a piece of string. If you have to constantly search for something to write with, you may lose the idea before you have time to write it down. Worse, you may tell yourself that you will remember your thought until you get home to your computer. You won't!

There's no right and wrong way to write down your ideas. You can use abbreviations, pictures, full phrases, quotes, or fragments—whatever helps you capture the thought and retain its relevance to your work. No one is going to be reading these notes but you, so feel free to use any kind of shorthand you want. The key is to make each note something you understand and can use.

Because you are ultimately going to organize these ideas, it is a good idea to separate them by story. For instance, you may come up with a strong title for your story but no other ideas. For now, write just the title on one page of your notebook and leave the rest of the page blank. If you later come up with character descriptions to go along with your title, flip back to that page and fill them in. If you capture feelings, descriptions, names, incidents, and bits of dialogue, add them to the page as well. Later on, when it comes time to actually write your story, consider how to connect these fragments. The richer your notes, the more cross-connections you'll think of.

Use outside sources to expand and grow your idea notebooks. Clip stories from newspapers, and write down web links, maps, drawings, and questions about your characters. Treat your notebooks as mini-scrapbooks of reference material

ESSENTIAL

Use sturdy notebooks that will stand up to use. Don't use pads that allow pages to curl, rip, and disappear. Use notebooks with covers, date them, and shelve them near your workstation.

You may find that you fill up notebooks quickly. In that case, you should start thinking about actually writing. It is easy to put off writing by using the excuse that you are still gathering material. But if you have several notebooks full, chances are you have a great story in there waiting to be written. Not every writer, not even every best-selling writer, is bursting with story ideas all the time. The next few sections explore different ways to rouse ideas and help you start filling up those notebooks.

Personal Experiences

Write what you know. How many times have you heard that? It can mean two things, each of which will be an important component of your work: write about experiences you have had, and write about things you have researched.

In Chapter 1 you were asked to create a timeline of significant events from your childhood. If you aren't sure where to start, use this to begin your journey. Recalling your own childhood is a great way to get your creative juices flowing. While significant events can certainly inspire plots, try to remember the insignificant things as well. One small detail has the power to shape an entire story.

Setting

Ideas for settings will be easy to come across if you consider your own childhood settings. Where did you grow up? Think about everything that surrounded you, from the items in your house to the geography of your location. Did you live in the country surrounded by forests and fields? Did you live in the city and play games in the streets with neighborhood kids? Were you landlocked or did you live on the water? Maybe you had a place you visited just to be by yourself—your own "secret garden." Think about why you chose that place, what elements it had that appealed to you.

What was the weather like? Maybe you grew up in tornado country. Maybe you lived on the coast and know what it's like to prepare for a hurricane. Did you have traditional activities relating to the seasons? Maybe you didn't even have seasons.

Try to recall everything you can about the setting in which you grew up. Can you create an atmosphere for a story from the background you knew so well as a child? While the setting in which you live now would be quite fine to work with, you won't know it from a child's perspective—unless of course you currently live where you grew up. Even more important than physical details of your childhood setting are the emotions you felt. When you write fiction the story may have little to do with your life, but the details and emotions you recall will make that story believable.

Emotions and Ideas

Try to recall specific emotions you had as a child and what actions triggered those emotions. For instance, perhaps you felt lonely when your big sister started school and you found yourself at home with no playmate. Maybe the death of a family member left you sad and confused. Can you remember the tingles of excitement as you tried to settle down for sleep on Christmas Eve?

ESSENTIAL

To help spark your memory, ask family members what you were like as a child. It will be fun and informative to hear their versions of events and compare them to your own. Another good idea is to take a look at photo albums of your younger years. The pictures may help you remember and piece together events.

Often children will build up an attachment to a particular item or habit. Maybe you had a blanket that you carried around with you constantly. Or perhaps you liked to twist your hair as a form of relaxation. How easy was it for you to give up your pacifier? Think about something you had an emotional attachment to and what it took to break you of the habit (that is, if you were able to break the habit).

The imagination of a child is something to be treasured. Try to recall your own young imagination. Did you invent a game for yourself and your siblings? Did you have an imaginary friend? Maybe you liked making up stories. Maybe you liked to pretend you were an astronaut. Make-believe is a child's way of exploring his creativity. Try to draw on your past encounters with make-believe to inspire creativity in your current stories.

Eyes Wide Open

Take a look around. The world is full of details just waiting to be picked up on and turned into a story. From major world events and issues to a phrase muttered by a child passing by on the street, there are millions of writing prompts in front of you. You just need to learn to open your eyes.

Walk down a familiar street and look for anything that is new or out of the ordinary. Maybe a tricycle was left in the driveway on its side. This may cause you to wonder why it wasn't put into the garage where it normally is. Was there an emergency at the house? Maybe the child was called in for lunch and isn't through riding the tricycle. Maybe the child is testing boundaries and seeing how far she can push her parents. Why was it left on its side? Maybe the child had exciting news to tell her parents and in her rush to get out of the seat, she knocked it over and didn't bother to pick it up. Maybe the child fell and, blaming the tricycle for the accident, got mad and kicked it until it tipped over. See, the mind can take just one small detail and run with it.

Train yourself to pay extra attention when you walk down the sidewalk. What are kids wearing? Notice the glances they give one another, the way they study adults, what a child says to his dog, or the color of a little girl's shoes. Whenever something catches your eye, consider it for a moment. Does it have story potential for you? If so, write it down in your notebook.

Have you ever sat on a train, noticed someone, and wondered what he did for a living or if he had any children or where he was going? If so, you were beginning to create a story about that person. Try this with a child. Pick out a child from a public place and watch her for a couple of minutes. Don't take any longer than that because you might raise the suspicions of a supervising adult; plus, you shouldn't need much time to get your mind in gear. Write down everything you make up about this child: name, hobbies, best friend, home life, age, favorite color, and so on. Don't concern yourself with story lines or plots just yet—unless that's what comes to mind. Right now you are just gathering ideas.

ESSENTIAL

The best way to heighten one of your senses is to shut off another. For instance, if you are searching for dialogue to add to your idea notebook, sit on a bench at a playground and shut your eyes. This will force you to listen to what's being said and how people use words to communicate.

Pay attention and use your imagination. You'll be surprised at the number of ideas that you come up with just by focusing on seemingly ordinary things. And don't forget to bring your notebook and write everything down!

Using the Media

While you may normally look to the media for entertainment or news, as a children's writer, you should try to train yourself to scan these sources for story material. Be careful, however, of watching television while writing. Writing requires intense concentration, and trying to engage your brain in a television program while attempting to write creatively and well will most likely lead to frustration. Each writer is different, however—some can listen to music while working, and others cannot; some can work in public places, like coffee shops, while others require complete isolation. Take your time, and learn what works for you.

The News

Some writers prefer to start from an item in the news, rather than from their own memory or observations. As you read the news on your favorite websites or in your daily newspaper, keep an eye out for anything that could serve as a plot, character, or setting. For instance, you might read a small article about a local lifeguard saving the life of a young boy. You might then write a story about a young girl who gets herself into trouble by disobeying her parents and sneaking off to go swimming. You explore her range of emotions as she finds herself in danger, throughout the rescue, and once she is safe. Or you might decide to write a story from the viewpoint of the lifeguard. Or you might disregard the people in the article altogether and simply choose to use a beach as your setting. From just one small article, your imagination can take over and suddenly you have several possibilities to jot down in your idea notebook. As you begin to imagine a story based on some else's life, your own experiences will add detail and emotion.

ALERT

Stealing other people's ideas and work is illegal. While it is perfectly okay to use the media to kindle your imagination, you should rely on your own creativity and writing ability to create a good story. Remember, you are just gathering material here. The actual story should be of your own making.

Classic Stories

You might find inspiration in reading classic and modern children's books. Read fairy tales, myths, legends, and folktales. Can you put a different spin on these? Maybe you can give the story a modern twist. Or you might choose to retell it from a different character's point of view. Consider researching the myths, legends, and fairy tales of different countries and cultures.

Music

Listen to songs on the radio and online. Disregard lyrics that simply repeat clichés, and pay attention to fresh, original songwriting. Do the lyrics describe a situation or discuss an issue that may translate into a story for children? Also listen to those songs that children find entertaining. Can you pinpoint why? Is there a universal message being sent that you could weave into a story line?

Advertisements

Even advertisements can inspire ideas. Take a closer look at billboards, posters, commercials, and ads in magazines and newspapers. Is there anything hidden there that might make for a good element in a children's book? What about those advertisements targeting children? How are these different and what makes them appealing to kids?

Organizing Your Ideas

Before you turn your ideas into stories, you should first get them organized. If you don't create an organizational system as you're gathering impressions, you may find yourself tackling a tower of paper when it comes time to use those ideas.

The same organizational system does not work for every person. Some people can't allow a single thing to be out of place before they begin work. Others have the messiest desk you've ever seen, but they know exactly where everything is. This section will give you some ideas, but you need to create an organizational system that you are comfortable with and that best suits your style.

First of all, you need some place to store the information and ideas you gather. A drawer or box dedicated to your children's book materials will work, as will a large envelope. The aim is to keep all your materials in one place so they are easily located. For the time being, you may find that your notebook works just fine. But chances are you will fill that notebook rather quickly and move on to the next. You need to organize those ideas so that they are easy to sift through.

A filing cabinet works best, but it isn't always reasonable to rush out and buy a huge filing cabinet, especially if you are just beginning to gather materials. If you have the space to devote to a filing cabinet, keep your eyes open for good deals. You can often find basic cabinets at office supply stores for a reasonable cost. You can also buy file cabinets from companies going out of business or at second-hand office supply stores.

FACT

Installing an organizational system for your ideas will save you time when you sit down to write. Organization also gives you a little peace of mind that will help to get and keep you motivated during the writing process.

To organize, you'll need to incorporate a filing system—whether it is for a filing cabinet, desk drawer, box, or a large envelope. If you can organize as you go, you will save yourself time. However, some people choose to organize their ideas only when they have a substantial number to work with.

Find a way to divide your ideas and related materials into categories. You may decide to separate the character ideas from the plot ideas, or the newspaper and magazine clippings from the notebook ideas. You may want to divide your ideas into type of book (fiction, nonfiction) or book format (picture book, early reader, chapter book, and so on). Do whatever works best for you, but be consistent.

It doesn't matter what type of organizational system you choose to use. The point is to make these materials easily accessible. If you leave loose papers lying around the house, chances are your ideas are going to be lost or turned into scrap paper for the kids to play with. Having worked so hard to gather ideas, you will want to take care of them. After all, one of them might just lead to your first book.

One at a Time

At some point you will want to write a story. Your idea collection may be the first place you look for inspiration. Now you will see what all the fuss was about—how all those hours spent gathering and sorting have saved your writing time!

It may be difficult to pick just one idea. As you pore through your collection, set aside those that are particularly appealing to you. When you go through this second pile, if not a single one stands out from the rest, you might just have to close your eyes and grab. Don't trouble yourself too much over this step. You'll explore those other ideas later on, so don't think of this as a final and all-important decision.

Read through your notes on your chosen idea, and jot down anything else that comes to mind. Start a new file for this one concept—it's going to be your main focus for a while.

What type of book is it going to be? Can you sketch out brief character descriptions? Can you follow the plot all the way through? If it is still an idea that you are excited about weeks after you initially thought of it, it may be strong enough to begin research.

ALERT

If you spend too much time gathering ideas, it is likely that your idea collection will be overflowing and this could create an intimidation factor that could affect your motivation to begin writing. Always keep your notebook handy, but know when it's time to change your focus.

If you are already having difficulty with it, are bored thinking about it, or don't think you'll ever be satisfied with it, toss it. You'll never be out of ideas, so keeping one around that isn't going to work for you is pointless and a waste of good idea space. If you just can't seem to let it go—maybe you're just not in the mood for that topic on that particular day, but feel that it does have potential—then set it aside in a separate file or envelope. Pick out a new idea from the collection and start over.

Research

When you have the idea you want to work with, it's time to do a little research—a lot of research if the topic is nonfiction. Use Internet search engines to find out what other books have been written on the same topic and take a look at these. Try a variety of key search words. Don't forget that the Internet is wide open, and anyone can post anything they want, true or not. Guard against faulty information by using primary sources as often as you can, and for secondary sources, sticking to trusted news organizations, such as the *New York Times*, and pages that end in .gov or .edu, which come from government or university websites.

For example, suppose you are writing a mystery about a twelve-year-old girl living in a small town. First, do some searches for "kid's mysteries," "children's mysteries," "girl detective," "middle-grade mysteries," "kid mystery authors," and "kid mystery publishers." These searches should lead you to some books you will want to read carefully. Cast a wide net in the beginning; look for anything that might be relevant in terms of target audience, and protagonist age (usually a couple of years older than the intended reading audience). Once you decide what the market is like for this kind of book, read some examples and make lists of qualities you admire and wish to avoid.

When you decide what your protagonist's town is like (its region, its size, and the way it feels), do searches to explore similar towns. If you can get to a town like the one you're describing, visit the local history section of the library and find books, often privately printed, about what that town was like in the past. The more you know about this town, the more vividly your town will spring to life on the page.

What about your protagonist's parents? Although they may not figure heavily in the story, it is still a good idea to know something about them. What do they do for a living? Search for stories in the newspaper or online about those professions and jobs. You can do a great deal of quality research using your computer.

QUESTION

What is a bibliography?
A bibliography lists the sources an author has referred to in researching and writing the book. The bibliography is normally found in the back of the book.

Talk to Specialists in the Field

You may decide to conduct interviews with specialists. Be courteous when asking for their time, and if they are too busy, don't take offense. Move on! When someone does sit down with you, have at least ten questions ready to ask. The more you already know about your project, the more specific the information you can request. But don't be too narrow in your focus, and do allow your interviewee to speak freely. You may hear stories or learn details that move your plot in a new direction.

Reference Materials

Your idea file will now turn into your new-book file, as it becomes a convenient place to store all of your reference materials. See why a filing cabinet was a good idea? Make sure to keep these materials in separate folders. Especially if you are writing nonfiction, you may need your sources and information later on.

If you are using reference materials at the library, make photocopies of the pages you refer to and write down the name of the book, author, publisher, publisher's location, and date of publication. While it may seem tedious now, it will be very time-consuming later if you write a bibliography and have to go back to each of your individual sources to retrieve the information you need.

CHAPTER 7

Writing Your Story

Now it's time to get to the heart of the matter: writing your story. This chapter helps you get started on your story, shows you how to keep the writing process flowing smoothly, and offers tips and advice to help you get past those obstacles every writer faces. Are you ready to write?

Getting Started

While it would certainly be nice to sit down and just let the story flow from your fingertips, most writers find that this rarely happens. Usually there is a lot of prep work to be done before the story begins. Don't be discouraged; the prep work can be a lot of fun and will make the actual writing advance smoothly.

First of all, you need to make sure your workstation is set up properly. Do you have your new-book file? Are your reference materials within reach? Do you have paper and pens? Are you comfortable? Try to eliminate all possibilities of distractions and interruptions. You need to focus on your work. You won't be able to concentrate if you have to get up and walk across the room for the dictionary constantly or if you are trying to eavesdrop on a television program on in the next room.

Read through your new-book file. Jot down any other ideas that pop into your head while you're reading. Don't ever assume that you will remember something. Your initial idea probably won't incorporate all the needed elements for a children's book; therefore you will need to sketch out an outline so you are sure of where you're going and can remain on track while writing.

Nonfiction

If you are writing a nonfiction book, you should have a well-defined topic. Be careful not to make the topic too broad. Narrow it down as much as possible and maintain your focus. You may want to write a one-sentence description of the book and put it up on the wall in front of you or on your computer—somewhere in your direct line of vision. If you ever feel yourself wavering from the main focus, read over your description again.

Before you begin writing, make sure you have all the sources you need within reach. If this involves several books, you may want to use sticky notes to mark specific passages or make notes. If you are especially industrious, you can use different colored sticky notes for your chapters. This will make referencing your sources quick and easy.

Your outline should be divided into chapters. Give each chapter a working title and list the points you want to cover in that chapter. You might find it helpful to give each chapter its own index card. (This also makes reorganizing easy.) When it comes time to write, you need only pull out that index card and you can concentrate solely on that chapter.

Remember that this is just an outline. It will help you organize your thoughts and develop your line of progression throughout the book. However, it doesn't mean that this outline is set in stone. As you conduct more thorough research, you may find that you need to alter the outline somewhat. Outlines may be very bare, medium in detail, or very detailed. Try all three to discover which works best for you.

Fiction

Fiction may be a little more difficult to sketch out; it's not quite as straightforward as nonfiction. Before you begin writing fiction you should answer the following questions:

- What will be the format of your book (picture book, early reader, chapter book, middle-grade, or young adult)?
- Who is this story about?
- What is his goal?
- What are his obstacles?
- Does this story fit your intended audience?
- Will you write in first person or third person?
- How will you begin your story?
- What happens in the middle of the story?
- How will you end your story?
- Will you write in past or present tense?
- Can you define the theme?
- Where does your story take place?

Again, try to come up with a one-sentence description and post it in view to help keep your focus. Answering the previous questions will certainly help you to begin writing, but there is one more thing you will need to know inside and out if you want to get your writing endeavor started off right: the characters.

The Characters

You need to know your characters intimately before beginning to write. It helps to think of your characters as real people instead of figments of your imagination. You should know what they look like, their likes and dislikes, any idiosyncrasies they may have, and their personality traits. If you believe your characters are real people, it will be easier to write them as real people.

FACT

Characters that are perfect are not realistic and normally do not work well in children's books (or adult books either, for that matter). All your characters should have weaknesses and flaws as well as strengths. Children want to relate to the characters in stories. If you create a perfect person, you will isolate that character, making him out of reach.

The Main Character

The main character should be the most in-depth character. Because this character will be the most developed, you may want to start off with this one. Running through the rest of the character descriptions will seem much easier once you have the main character sketched out. Plus, the secondary characters may very well play off of the main character in regard to their functions in the story.

Figure out as much as you possibly can about your main character before writing; don't expect it all to come to you as you go along. Create a character description by answering the following questions as well as any others you can think of that will help define your character:

- What is the character's name?
- What is the character's gender?
- What does the character look like (hair and eye color, height, weight, distinguishing features, and so on)?
- How old is the character?
- What are the character's pet peeves?
- What are the character's hobbies?
- What are the character's relationships to the secondary characters?

- What are the character's strengths?
- What are the character's weaknesses?
- Where is the character's setting (house, school, city, country)?
- Who are the character's friends?
- What is the character's family like?

Your main character is the one who will grow and develop throughout the book. Do you have a game plan for this growth progress? It isn't acceptable to simply have the character suddenly come up with the correct solution and end the story happily ever after. You will need to show how the character struggles with her progress, how she overcomes obstacles, and the thought process along the way.

ALERT

Stay away from making your characters inanimate objects. While it has certainly been done, editors usually cringe when reading a manuscript in which an inanimate object such as a couch or refrigerator suddenly comes to life and can walk and talk.

Secondary Characters

Your secondary characters don't need to be as detailed as your main character. However, they are still essential to the story, so you should know them well before you start writing. You'll need to know the names, ages, and physical descriptions of these characters, as well as their relationships to the main character. Do you need to know their personal strengths and weaknesses? It will help, even if you don't reveal these traits explicitly in your book. If you know the deep background of all your characters, your readers will feel it.

Because these characters won't be as evident as the main character, it sometimes helps to give each one an individual quirk or habit that will help both you and your reader recognize and distinguish the character a little better. For instance, maybe your main character has a four-year-old sister who is constantly sucking her thumb. Or maybe the main character's best friend is superstitious and is always on the lookout for bad and good omens.

Use your creativity to keep these characters from being only pawns in the story. Though they may not be as important as the main character, they still deserve their own identity.

You will also want to stay away from stereotypes. It is easy to give in to the temptation, but editors are looking for fresh and original characters. For instance, if you find yourself using that kind old lady doling out cookies and milk to the neighborhood kids, give her a flaw that will take away from her seeming perfection. Maybe her cookies are often salty instead of sugary because she is always misplacing her glasses. No one is perfect and if you want to make your characters believable, you'll have to recognize that in your character descriptions.

Developing Character's Voices

While your characters should each have a different voice, you need to establish your main character's voice before starting out to write. This will put the finishing touches on knowing your main character inside and out.

A good way to find your character's voice is to create a mock journal in which your character writes daily. Because a journal is personal, your character will feel free to write what he feels without worrying about outside opinions. Create a week's worth of journal entries for your character. This should be sufficient to identify a style and voice that is all his or her own.

ESSENTIAL

Another exercise you might try to find your character's voice is to have the character write a short autobiography. This will force you to have the character speak in her own words and will help you to establish a background for this character.

Remain consistent with your secondary characters throughout. However, let characters be surprising at times, and let your main character grow. After a crisis, you want readers to feel your people acted at their best or worst, consistent with the potential that was hinted at earlier.

Writing Dialogue

Using dialogue helps keep the text fresh and stimulating. For those learning to read, the use of dialogue also provides white space on the page without seeming to purposely give the reader a break. For these younger readers, white space is often a relief to see.

Writing dialogue is a skill worthy of practice. You want your dialogue to help move the story along and sound natural at the same time. It should have a purpose. A unique line of dialogue displays values and intelligence—in short, it reveals character.

One of the most difficult tasks a writer faces is making dialogue sound natural. The best way to achieve this is to listen to what people say and how they say it. How do children speak to each other compared to how they speak to adults? Do the conversations among girls differ from those among boys? What about the conversations between boys and girls? Pay close attention to the dialogue in well-reviewed books written for your target age group. Most importantly, your characters should have a way of speaking that fits the world of your book. They should not sound as if they were recorded on a playground; while sounding natural, their speech should reveal their unique intentions and fears.

Realistic Speech Styles

Pay attention to grammar and style. Children do not always speak in complete sentences, and if you consistently use complete sentences in your dialogue, it will probably sound unnatural. You will also find that people stammer, use the wrong word, pause while searching for what to say next, and repeat themselves over and over. You don't need to reproduce these verbal habits in your writing. While they are natural styles, they can also be very distracting. Would you really like to read the same sentence five times in a row?

Use your best judgment and focus on the purpose of the dialogue. If a speech style helps to define your character or move the story along, then you can certainly use it. But keep in mind that overhearing real people and reading about fictional people are two different things. Allow your reader to tune out boring speech, just as he might in a normal conversation. Focus instead on speech that moves your story forward.

Your characters will speak differently depending on their personalities. You may have a shy girl who hardly says a word at all and an outgoing boy who loudly expresses his opinion on everything. Match up speech patterns with personality traits. Children speak differently in different regions, and differently from each other—even from family members and friends. Make use of this in your story to help the reader delineate the individual characters and better understand them.

FACT

The only way you can tell if your dialogue sounds natural is to read it aloud or have someone else read it to you. This will also help you to get to know your characters better. Read the conversations as though you were acting out the part of each individual character.

Using Correct Language

You must be careful to not write your dialogue *exactly* as it is spoken. People sometimes run their words together or leave off endings. For instance, you may hear the word "gonna" used frequently, but it is often best to translate it into "going to" in your work. If you are writing for young readers, you don't want to lead them away from correct language while they are still learning. Even if you are writing for advanced readers who know better, it is still best to use correct language.

If dialect is required to develop your character or story, use it sparingly. A little goes a long way to suggest a speech pattern. Instead of misspellings, use colorful expressions like "tuckered out" or "dag nabbit." Avoid clichés and invent your own expressions, such as "he was plum tummy full" or "she was mad enough to bite."

Years ago, writers often used phonetic spelling to represent words used in dialect. For example, a writer might have indicated the words "it sure doesn't" by writing "it sho dont"—without an apostrophe. There are two reasons to avoid this practice. First, it is difficult to use phonetic spelling accurately for dialect you didn't grow up with. And second, if your characters are smart, phonetic spellings will make them seem less so. This practice may also suggest class, social, or racial snobbery and can reinforce cultural stereotyping.

Identifying Speakers

When writing dialogue, you also must be sure to identify the speakers. No one wants to retrace a conversation to figure out who is speaking. If you write straightforward conversation between only two people, it isn't necessary to tag each line. But if it goes on for a while, you will need to identify the characters every few lines just to keep things straight. Also be sure to start a new paragraph with each new speaker.

ALERT

While you want your dialogue to sound natural, try to stay away from using current trendy phrases. This will date your book and label it relevant only to those children of today. If your story is packed with popular sayings, it will be inaccessible to children forty years from now.

Using the word *said* is perfectly acceptable for a tag line. Don't feel as though you must substitute a variety of words for said. Using too many adverbs or an assortment of said synonyms will weigh down the dialogue. People are used to plain old said and can easily read through it without having to grasp any more than the identity of the speaker.

Show and Tell

If you take a writing class, the "show, don't tell" suggestion will almost always be brought up. This applies to children's writing especially. Because you are writing for children, you want to write action-packed stories. This doesn't necessarily mean you need burning buildings and extreme drama. But you should always have something happening that advances the story of the main character struggling against obstacles to attain her goal. A good way to keep the story moving is to show the action instead of simply stating that something happened.

As a writer, you must always allow your reader to figure out some things on his own, especially when it comes to understanding what a character is feeling. Children are smart and capable readers and are up to this challenge. For instance, instead of simply stating, "Amy is shy," show Amy standing alone in a corner, biting her nails, glancing around, yet avoiding eye contact. Your readers will understand—maybe all too well—what Amy is feeling.

Showing, through dialogue and description, is important, but so is telling, through narrative summary. Showing an action unfold draws readers close to the characters. Moments of narrative reflection allow your characters and your readers to pause and consider the meanings of events that have happened thus far in your story.

Using the Active Voice

Another good rule of thumb is to choose the active voice over the passive voice whenever you can. This makes the text more stimulating and gives it an effect of movement.

If you use the passive voice too often, the text seems lifeless and static. For example, compare the two sentences below. Which is more lively and better suited for a children's book?

The vase was shattered to pieces after it was thrown by Mary.

Mary threw the vase and shattered it to pieces.

The first sentence uses a passive voice, which tells the reader what has happened. The second sentence uses an active voice, which shows the action. Can you tell the difference? The passive voice normally uses a form of the verb *to be*, such as *is*, *was, are,* or *were.* The active voice uses action verbs such as *throw, hide, run,* and *sneeze.* If showing versus telling is still unclear, write a story using only the passive voice. Then write the same story using an active voice. Read them both aloud and you should be able to hear a distinct difference between the two.

Writing Tips

As you well know, writing for children is no easy task. You can learn only so much from reading how-to books, and the rest you will have to learn on your own.

If you are writing your very first book, you might feel overwhelmed at the moment. It will get easier as you get into the habit of writing regularly and progress with several works. Don't feel as if you are alone out there. Writing for children isn't easy for anyone, even seasoned authors. Keep the following tips in mind; they will help you throughout the writing process:

- **Concentrate.** Relaxed concentration is the key to writing well. You won't be able to focus on your work if you have outside factors distracting you.
- **Omit unnecessary words.** Children's books normally don't allow a lot of room for text, so you must make the very best of the space you have. Make every word count.
- **Don't use clichés.** Your text should be fresh and original. Most editors consider the use of clichés to be lazy writing.
- **Watch your tenses.** Don't start a story in present tense and finish in past tense.
- **Create smooth transitions.** The lack of transitional phrases or sentences will make your text sound choppy and confusing.
- **Take breaks.** If you schedule several hours of writing time, you need to take short breaks frequently. Stand, stretch, take a short walk, or anything else you can think of to take you away from the stresses of sitting in one position staring at a computer screen.
- **Keep the number of characters to a minimum.** The fewer characters you have, the more room you have to go in-depth with each. A large number of characters will most likely confuse the reader.
- **Don't go overboard with descriptions.** Use descriptions that are necessary to the story line, and let the readers use their imaginations for the rest.
- **Don't preach.** You can certainly convey an important message through your story, but don't tell your readers what to think.
- **Begin your story with action.** You want to hook your readers with the very first line. If you spend time in the beginning describing the setting and giving the backgrounds of your characters, readers will get bored, put the book down, and never pick it up again.

- **Balance description, dialogue, and narration in your story.** Description makes readers believe, dialogue brings them in close, and narration supplies meaning.

Writer's Block

Nearly all writers suffer writer's block at some point during their lives—some even do so on a regular basis. Writer's block is simply that period of time when you stare blankly at your work without writing a single word. Your inspiration seems to have flown out the window and your brain has shut down. Writer's block can be very frustrating and will test your aptitude for writing. But you can't let it get the best of you. You are the one with the fantastic ideas and wonderful talent. Just as any job has obstacles, so does writing: writer's block is an obstacle that you will need to overcome.

ESSENTIAL

To make the best use of your allotted writing time and to help alleviate writer's block, schedule your writing time during your most productive time of day. For instance, if you are most creative during the early morning, get up an hour earlier and schedule that time to write.

The Root of the Problem

To overcome writer's block, you need to get to the root of the problem. Try to figure out what is causing you to stall. While there are several possibilities, quite often writer's block is caused by one of two things: fear or stress.

Whether you are just beginning or are a seasoned author, fear can get in the way of your writing. Perhaps you are afraid of this new venture and believe that you are not good enough to make it. Maybe you have been successful with a past book and are afraid your next is not going to meet the high standards set by your audience and publisher. The good news is, writing is often about facing your fears. You can draw energy from creatively combating what bothers you.

Another common source of writer's block is stress. Perhaps you are working under a tight deadline. Maybe you have three children screaming in the background while you are trying to work. Or you may have a relative who is ill and who you can't stop thinking about. Try to identify sources of stress affecting your ability to write.

Of course, fear and stress aren't the only factors that can affect your work, but they are good starting points if you are unsure of what is causing writer's block. Once you know what the root of the problem is, you can then take steps to overcome it.

Overcoming Writer's Block

One of the first things you'll want to try is to just write. Start typing. Don't worry about quality—just use this time to get into your story. Many writers start each writing session this way and eventually throw out the first page. By the second, they have often found their groove and the quality returns to their sentences.

If you are just simply stuck and can't think of any particular reason why you are suffering writer's block, you may want to try some writing exercises that will loosen you up and take the pressure off of writing a particular story. For instance, try a free-writing exercise in which you simply write whatever comes to mind. Don't concentrate on anything and don't stop to think, just write. This may loosen you up, produce notes for a future story, and allow you to return to your book with a more relaxed concentration.

ESSENTIAL

Sometimes writer's block hits so hard that your only option is to temporarily abandon the story. While this may be necessary, don't ignore your daily writing schedule. Use that time to work on another story idea, compose a letter to a friend, or write in your journal.

You might also try a change of scenery. Maybe you have worked so many hours in a small corner of the house that you are beginning to feel suffocated and antsy without even realizing it. Grab a notebook and pencil and walk to the park or a coffee shop to write. A breath of fresh air may be just the cure for your bout with writer's block.

Or perhaps looking at books will inspire you. Pay a visit to your local library. Wander through the stacks, looking over books of various kinds. Have your pencil and paper ready and jot down anything that occurs to you. You never know where and when inspiration will strike.

CHAPTER 8

Revising Your Story

So you've completed your story and are anxious to send it off to a publisher. Stop right there. You have reached a difficult goal, but you're not done yet. Your manuscript will need several rounds of revision before it is fit for submission. Editors do not welcome first drafts; luckily for you, in addition to being a critical part of the writing process, revision can be fun.

Distancing Yourself

Completing a book is a great feeling. Undoubtedly you worked very hard to take a fragment of an idea and turn it into a completed manuscript, full of life and color. But even though you may be itching to submit your manuscript to a publisher, you need to first look it over with a critical eye. You want your manuscript to be as close to perfect as it can be before you let an editor see it.

To be able to critique yourself, you will have to distance yourself from the manuscript. Pretend that you are reading someone else's work. Try your best to clear your mind of your manuscript and look at it with a fresh eye. This will be rather difficult, but if you concentrate on separating yourself it will get easier as you progress.

Revision is a multistage process. Before you begin, it may help to read through your manuscript, and then take a step back from it. Let it sit with you for a while. Take the time you need—a few weeks, a month even. When you pick the manuscript back up, you will be able to read it more objectively.

The First Read-Through

You will read through your manuscript several times before it is ready for submission. During each stage you must concentrate on a different area of revision. If re-reading a certain portion of your book is unappealing, you probably need to revise.

ESSENTIAL

Keep an eye out for typos. If you submit a manuscript with typos, the editor probably won't waste his time reading it all the way through. Editors are looking only for those writers who are serious about their work.

During the first stage, focus only on the content of the book. Do any questions pop into your head while reading? Are there any holes that need to be filled? Are you consistent with your characters? Has your main character grown and developed throughout the book? Does each scene tie in to the plot? Are you able to visualize the setting and each scene? Is your writing original and fresh or have some clichés slipped in?

Consider creating a list of questions like these before reading through your manuscript. If you know what you are looking for before you begin reading, you have a better shot at catching content errors and noticing areas that need to be revised.

The Second Read-Through

Once you're satisfied with the overall content, you need to read the manuscript one sentence at a time. Though you may wonder how you normally read if it isn't one sentence at a time, this is different. You will read one sentence, stop, and consider only that sentence.

Are there any words in that sentence that you could omit without losing its meaning? Because children's books have precious little space to work with, it is especially important to omit needless words. Can you improve on the sentence structure? Can you make the sentence more concise and clear? Does the sentence say *exactly* what you want it to say? Are you using an active voice?

When you have answered all these questions (as well others you come up with) for the individual sentence, consider that sentence's relationship to those surrounding it. Is it in the best place? Does it maintain the rhythm and flow of the text or is it jarring and different from the rest? Do you want it to stand out?

ALERT

Don't rely on your computer's spell check feature to catch all spelling mistakes. Some words may be spelled correctly but used incorrectly. For instance, the spell checker won't pick up on the incorrect use of *to, two,* and *too* since all are spelled correctly.

While it may seem daunting (and time-consuming!) to put so much consideration into one sentence at a time, know that this will not only benefit the finished product but also help you write better in the future.

The Third Read-Through

Once you have completed the first and second read-throughs and made the appropriate changes, read through your manuscript one more time, focusing only on grammar, punctuation, and spelling. Keep a dictionary and a style manual close by.

Are paragraphs divided where they should be? Have you placed speakers' words in quotation marks? Do you have too many exclamation points? Are commas in the right place? The checklist for grammar, punctuation, and spelling is endless, but you know best in which areas you are a bit weak and what to look out for. For instance, if you have a tendency to confuse *its* with *it's* (which is a common mistake), take care to double check these throughout the manuscript. You may want to keep a list of commonly misspelled words close by as well as a personal checklist of difficulties you may have.

Testing One, Two, Three

While critiquing your own work is certainly necessary, sometimes it helps to get an outside opinion. Would you rather your first outside opinion be that of an editor who has the ability to reject your manuscript for publication, or that of someone who will help you catch its flaws before it is up for consideration? While you certainly have authority over your manuscript, you might find it helpful to test out your manuscript on one or all of the following groups of people.

Call on Your Friends

What are friends for if not to lend a helping hand? Your close friends and family will most likely share in your excitement as you complete a manuscript, and those who have time may be willing to read it over. This can be one of the most beneficial reads you get, since it will likely be the first time the book is being read by someone other than you. Just keep in mind that friends have an emotional tie to you that may get in the way of their objectivity.

You may find it more comfortable to allow friends and family, as opposed to a stranger or someone you don't know well, read your work. Your friends aren't likely to say bad things about the manuscript and will be much more gentle than an editor in telling you it needs more work. Make it clear from the start that you *want* criticism. Ask them to praise what they admire first, then give you honest suggestions for improvement.

Turn to Your Writers' Group

If you belong to a writers' group, take advantage of it! The members are there to help one another in their writing endeavors. This is the perfect forum for feedback on your completed (or so you thought) manuscript. The members will have varying levels of experience and expertise, and you should get a variety of suggestions and advice.

ESSENTIAL

Open yourself up to criticism and welcome it. Accepting criticism may be quite difficult at this stage, considering you have put so much time and effort into producing a manuscript that you thought was flawless. Just remember that criticism will help you see things you may have missed because you are too close to the work.

Listen to their comments carefully and take notes. It is likely that they will pick up on problems you have skimmed over or turned a blind eye to. Hopefully, the group will praise you for good work and then give you constructive criticism. Praise alone won't help you get published, but neither will a blow to your self-esteem.

The True Test: Children

If at all possible, test your manuscript on your intended audience: children. What's so great about this test group is that not only are you going to receive feedback from those you have worked so hard to reach out to, but you are most likely going to receive the honest and blunt criticism that your friends and fellow adults may be reluctant to give.

Reading your book to the children in your family will certainly help, but keep in mind that like your family and friends, these children have a connection with you and their feedback will probably be biased. They may seem to enjoy the book when really they are mainly enjoying spending time with you. If at all possible, read your manuscript to a group of children who don't know you. Ask a local school, library, or daycare center for permission to read your book during story time.

Your very best option would be to have another adult read your story to a group of children while you sit by and observe. This will allow you to hear your story as it would likely be read and to pay attention to the body language of the children without the distraction of reading yourself.

It's a good idea to have a list of questions on hand to ask the group of children once the story is finished. Getting the answers to simple questions such as whether or not they liked the story or what their favorite part was can tell you a lot about how your story affected them. How did they react when the story was being told—did they squirm? Did they yawn or even fall asleep? Did they lean forward and pay attention to certain parts? Did they look around during certain parts? Did they sit through the entire story with a look of amazement on their faces? Did they ask to have it read again?

Hiring an Editor

There comes a time in every writer's life when he is just not sure about the manuscript. It may have gone through several critiques and rewrites, but some unseen force is holding the writer back from submitting it to an agent or publisher. This may be the perfect time to call on the help of a professional.

There are many freelance children's book editors out there who will charge a fee to give your manuscript the benefit of a professional and experienced eye. The advantage of this is that you will likely hire someone who doesn't have a personal connection with you and can give your work an unbiased critique; plus these editors work with children's authors on a regular basis and know what makes a children's book publishable and successful.

However, if you choose to take this route, you should be careful to find an editor who is reputable and specializes in children's books. Unfortunately, there are a lot of scam artists who will charge you to evaluate your manuscript without telling you what you need to know. They may send a very general and vague form letter that does not specifically address issues in your manuscript. If they even read your manuscript, chances are you aren't going to get the feedback you require.

The Search Begins

Start by asking around. Try to find someone who has had firsthand experience with a freelance editor. This is another opportunity to use social networking to your advantage. Post to your Facebook and Twitter accounts that you are seeking a freelance editor for some help with your children's book manuscript. There are thousands of these people available online, some more worthwhile than others, but it is best to begin with personal recommendations.

ALERT

Beware of advertisements that promise to get you published. Unless you are dealing with one of the many reputable self-publishing firms from which you buy specific services that are clearly spelled out, chances are you will pay exorbitant amounts of money and get nothing in return.

Ask the members of your writers' group. If nothing turns up, try a Google search. You should not give any editor an up-front fee before checking her references. Does she claim to be a university professor? Check with the school. Does she claim to have worked with best-selling authors? Ask for personal references from them. If you prefer to work with someone local, try contacting the English or writing departments at your local colleges and universities. Ask if anyone on the faculty is interested in some freelance editing work.

Do Your Homework

Once you get a name, you should do some research of your own. Before you contact the editor, do a little background check. What books has she worked on? Are these books self-published or are they published through a publishing house?

If your contact meets your satisfaction through this first phase, schedule a time to meet or chat with the editor. Put together a list of questions and don't let her sidestep them. If you are expected to pay for a consultation, the editor will certainly understand your need for knowledge about her working credentials. If the editor refuses to provide them or can't answer your questions, this should raise a red flag.

ESSENTIAL

If you attend writers' groups, conferences, or seminars, you may have the opportunity to hear a professional editor speak. If you liked what was said, try to speak with this editor following the meeting. He may have an interest in critiquing your manuscript or know of a freelance editor with a good reputation.

Try to find out the editor's past and current work experience, method of consultation, summary of charges, and current workload (a busy editor might not be able to get to your manuscript for several months). It is also a good idea to get a list of references and check them out.

Learning When to Let Go

Some writers get so caught up in the revision process that the end is never in sight. Sometimes the story goes through so many revisions that it does not even resemble the original idea. Maybe the new stuff is better—in which case, job well done. But maybe the new stuff is just *different.* You want to make your story the best it can be, but you also have to know when to say when.

The Perfectionist

If you are a perfectionist, letting go will be hard for you. After several revisions, you may have a great idea that you believe will finally complete your story. You make the change. You read back through the manuscript and bask in its perfection, then discover that the change you made requires other changes to the manuscript for reasons of consistency. Sighing, you make the other changes only to find that the story has taken a different path and doesn't read nearly as well as it did in the first place.

Never fear, the cycle can be broken. First, give yourself a deadline. Write it down in your planner, stick a note to your computer, write it in big red letters on the wall—do whatever it takes to make the deadline real. If you convince yourself that you absolutely must meet that deadline, your mind will start prioritizing for you. You will find that suddenly your use of grammar becomes more important than changing the hair color of a secondary character.

Next, meet your deadline. If you have to strap yourself to a chair in front of your computer for sixteen hours a day, do it. You must not, under any circumstances, go beyond your deadline. The perfectionist in you will ensure that your spelling, grammar, punctuation, and other essential elements are met to the best of your abilities before you reach that deadline. You will gradually learn to let go of those things that are not essential to your story and resist the temptation to rewrite a hundred times.

Stuck on a Phrase

You may discover during the revision process that your favorite phrase—the very phrase the entire book was written around—needs to be cut. This phrase was part of the book from the very beginning. It was the first thing you added to the idea file. You love the phrase—it's a work of genius; it rolls off your tongue to charm all those who hear it; it sums up everything you want to say in just a few simple words.

The phrase haunted you day and night, trying to worm its way into a story. Finally, you were able to use it to create a story. However, as you read back through your work, you find that the story has taken on a life of its own, and the phrase no longer fits. So what do you do? Well, the story is more important than the phrase, so cut it and move on.

ALERT

If you have to cut a favorite phrase from a story, don't throw it away! Place the phrase back in your idea files and try to find a way to use it elsewhere. This way, the heartache will be less severe and you will be able to create more stories from the phrase.

You could delete most of the story itself and try to rework it to fit in with the beloved phrase. Or you could do what you know is best, though it pains you, and cut the phrase from the story. Let it go and know that you have made a proper sacrifice to the craft of writing.

Revision Checklist

While each children's book is different, there are some general things you want to keep in mind while making your revisions. Use the following list of questions to help you along with the process, but don't rely solely on this list. Also make those revisions that are specific to your story.

1. Is the plot appropriate for the age level you are targeting?
2. Has your main character grown and developed throughout the story?
3. Is the manuscript's length appropriate for the age level you are targeting?
4. Have you spell checked your work?
5. Are your characters consistent throughout?
6. Is your story constantly moving?
7. Have you used dialogue to move the story along or help describe characters?
8. Have you omitted needless words?
9. Have you verified all facts?
10. Does the opening hook the reader?
11. Are your grammar and punctuation correct?
12. Does the main character solve the problem?
13. Have you kept your descriptions in check and left some things up to the imagination of the reader?
14. Have you used the active voice instead of the passive voice?
15. Are you consistent with point of view?
16. Are you consistent with tenses?
17. Have you removed all dated material from the manuscript?
18. Does the dialogue sound natural?
19. Does every character have a distinct identity?
20. Does the manuscript read smoothly?

It's Your Story

Yes, you need to revise. Yes, you should seek the help of others. Yes, you should consider all that they say. No, you don't have to change anything. What you need to keep in mind throughout the entire revision process is that this story is yours and yours alone.

Trust Your Instincts

You are the author and you are in control. People may certainly add their two cents' worth and it may be worth two dollars, but unless you feel that their comments change your story for the better and you are comfortable making that change, take it only as opinion.

ESSENTIAL

You must believe in yourself and your writing abilities if you want to make it through the revision process unscathed. Don't lose sight of your goals, your motivation for writing, and your love of the story. View everything as part of the learning process and remember that editing improves your work.

If you feel that your story is the very best it can be, though others are telling you to change this or that, go with your instincts. Find a publishing company, prepare your manuscript for submission, and send it in.

Editorial Revisions

Almost every book that reaches the shelves will have undergone editorial revisions. While you have certainly put in tons of work and time writing and rewriting, an editor will most likely want to revise even more. Keep in mind that while you are writing for your own purposes and are attempting to create great literature, an editor is trying to convince the publisher that your book will bring in money for the company.

Let's say you have sent in a manuscript. You get a call from the editor and she tells you she likes the book. Your heart skips a beat. But then she says that she can't buy the book until it has been revised. Are you willing to do the revisions? Thinking that you may have left in a typo or spelled a word incorrectly, you agree. You receive the manuscript back and find an eight-page editorial memo outlining the extensive revisions that need to be made before the company will purchase your book. So what do you do?

You have two options. One, you can do the extensive revisions and give your manuscript a solid chance of being published. Two, you can take your manuscript elsewhere and begin the submission process all over again. The choice is up to you; after all, the story is yours.

However, before you make your decision, you should consider a few things. The children's publishing industry is very competitive. If you pull your manuscript from this editor, she will undoubtedly have another one waiting to take its place. If you stay with this editor, there is no guarantee you will be published, but the editor obviously saw something she liked, so you have a good shot at it. Also, keep in mind that wherever you take your manuscript, any interested editor will likely insist on changes before it is published.

CHAPTER 9

Putting Pictures to Words

Many children's books rely on illustrations to help tell the story. But who draws those illustrations and how are they chosen to accompany a particular book? Whether you are a writer without the ability to draw a recognizable stick figure or a professional illustrator trying your hand at writing, this chapter will help you better understand the process of putting pictures to words.

To Be or Not to Be an Illustrator

Aspiring writers sometimes mistakenly assume that they need to provide illustrations for their picture books. Having looked at the variety of amazing illustrations in children's books today, you probably find this notion very intimidating. If you are a writer and not an illustrator, there is no need to worry—most often, publishers take on the responsibility of finding an illustrator for books they publish. If you believe you have the ability to illustrate your own work, you may well have the opportunity to do so, but you need to take a close look at your artwork before choosing to submit it.

ALERT

It's a good idea to visualize illustrations to accompany your text while writing. This will help you see if you are creating a well-rounded story. However, just because you can visualize pictures to go along with your story doesn't mean you can draw them, nor does it mean that those images will or should accompany your text.

What Are Your Qualifications?

If you want to submit illustrations for your book, think about your qualifications. Because writing and illustrating are looked upon as two separate talents, you need to be able to prove that you are adept at both. Do you have a degree from an art school? Have you published other illustrations? Does your work stand up to professional standards?

Publishers often view writers and illustrators as separate people with separate skills, so if you are eager to illustrate your own book, you will have to convince the publishing company that you are the best artist for the job. You must realize that you will be in competition with other professional illustrators.

Assessing Your Skill

If you still believe that you are the best person to illustrate your book, browse through a variety of children's books from those publishers that may potentially publish your book and pay close attention to the illustrations.

How does your artwork compare to these published illustrations? While these artists certainly have their own individual styles, they may also have a common quality that was imposed by the publisher. Can you pinpoint what that quality is? Will you be able to alter your style to fit in with the style of the publishing company?

ESSENTIAL

It helps to get an outside opinion when assessing your skill as an illustrator. Consider showing your artwork to a critique group or hiring a professional illustrator to take a look at your work and provide feedback.

Aside from meeting a specific publishing company's needs, does your artwork suit children's books in general? For instance, consider whether you are able to capture exactly what is needed to move the story along. Do your drawings have too much action taking place, or not enough? Will your work appeal to children? Would you be able to illustrate a book other than your own? You will need to convince the publisher of your skill as an illustrator separate from that as a writer.

Presenting Your Work

If you decide that you are quite capable of producing professional illustrations and want to take a shot at illustrating a children's book (whether your own or others'), then you need to present your work in a professional manner to increase your chances of acceptance. There are a couple of different ways you can go about this.

Petitioning the Editor

If you want to illustrate your own book, you may decide to send samples of your artwork along with the manuscript to an editor. Let the editor know in the cover letter that you are interested in illustrating your own book. You will probably want to include both color and black-and-white sketches to show your range of ability. Remember, these are just samples.

Of course you will want to present your best work, but do not illustrate the entire book at this time.

You can also create a dummy book to send in to an editor. A dummy is a mock-up of a real book. Be sure to create the correct number of pages (for instance, allow thirty-two pages for a picture book) and leave room for the front matter. Break up the text from the manuscript and paste it on the appropriate pages. This will also help you, as a writer, to see if your text flows well from page to page and whether you have too much or too little text.

Once you have the text pasted onto the dummy, it is time to add the illustrations. You should prepare a couple of finished pieces to show your ability as an illustrator. You can use sketches to represent the remaining illustrations. Keep a copy of the dummy for your files.

ALERT

When sending in samples of your artwork, *never* send the original art. If you send in original art, you run the risk of losing it in the mail or never having it returned, plus you will look like an amateur for doing so. It's best to be on the safe side and send in photocopies instead.

A dummy not only shows your ability as an illustrator, but it also shows that you understand very well the concept and design of a picture book. However, keep in mind that you should submit a dummy only if you are confident that you have the ability to be both a writer and an illustrator. You certainly don't want an editor's opinion of your artwork to be less than first-rate, as it may adversely affect the editor's impression of your writing.

Contacting the Art Director

If you have a burning desire to illustrate children's books, you should send samples to the art director. The art director is normally the person who decides who will be added to the illustrator roster. As a professional illustrator, you should have a portfolio available should the art director want to see more of your work.

Submitting artwork to a publishing house requires just as much research as does submitting a manuscript. Spend a lot of time with current children's books. Can you distinguish traits that are specific to individual publishing companies? Can you tell what it is that they are looking for in an illustrator? Choose to contact publishing companies that produce picture books in line with your style of illustration.

ESSENTIAL

In addition to the wealth of information the Children's Book Council provides to writers, it also offers information for illustrators. Contact this organization and request a copy of *An Illustrator's Guide to Members of the Children's Book Council*, which will provide you with information to help you get your foot in the door.

When sending in samples of your artwork, make sure you have the correct contact name, send along a self-addressed stamped envelope, include a cover letter, and above all, follow the publishing company's submission guidelines! If you want to become an illustrator of children's books, you need to distinguish yourself as an illustrator, not just an author who happens to be able to draw. The best way to do this is to approach the art department in a professional manner and present your very best work, leaving the author side of you at home.

Publisher's Choice

If you don't have the ability to illustrate your story, then who will illustrate it for you? Because the illustrations are very important to your children's book, you want to know that they will be a perfect match. Maybe you have a good friend who likes to draw and just know that the two of you will be able to work together to create an awesome picture book. Or perhaps you are considering hiring a professional illustrator to make sure the work is of the highest quality. Stop right there. Even though it may seem logical—after all, your book will need pictures, and who better than the author will know what needs to be drawn?—you do not need to submit illustrations with your work to an editor, nor should you. Submitting art (that is not yours) to an editor screams out "amateur" and will adversely affect the way the editor views your writing.

In most cases, the publisher hires the illustrator. Sometimes a publishing company will have a select group of artists who are used consistently to maintain a house style. Other times, a publishing company will hire artists on a book-by-book basis depending on what style fits well with what book. You, as the writer, are not likely to be included in the choice of illustrator. This is something you will just have to accept. But take heart: publishers are in the business of creating and selling books, so they know what they're doing.

Even though the illustrations are an integral part of your story, try to think of illustrating as just another process your book needs to go through to reach the end result. You wouldn't want the responsibility of choosing the printer, would you? Trust the expertise and experience of the publishing company to produce the best results. It is the company's job to recognize what sells and to make its books (and yours) stand up to and surpass the competition.

Once your manuscript leaves your hands, it will be open to interpretation by others. An illustrator's vision may differ from yours, as may an editor's. Some elements of the pictures will be fresh ideas from the artist, rather than from your text. If you want to be successful in the field of children's publishing, you will open yourself to the opinions of these professionals. You may just be pleasantly surprised with the results, even though the pictures stray quite a distance from what you originally imagined.

Also keep in mind that if you create a fuss about not having any say in the choice of illustrator, it is likely that an editor will find you difficult to work with and think twice before hiring you to write another book. Publishing is a business, and in order to be successful you need to recognize that a team effort is required to sell a book. If you are a good team player and trust in the abilities of the professionals, you will be able to relax and find enjoyment in knowing your book will reach the hands of children.

Remember that regardless of who illustrates the book and what the pictures look like, the story is still yours.

Working with the Illustrator

When you write a picture book, you envision certain visual elements—some more clearly than others. For instance, because you need to get to know your characters intimately in order to make them seem real to readers, you must have a picture of them in your mind. If the setting is detailed and crucial to the story, you will certainly have a picture of this as well. However, most writers do not see the pictures in their mind transferred to the page. Maybe you can't possibly fathom that your book would work illustrated in any other way than what you have imagined. In which case, you should provide detailed instructions for the illustrator, right? Wrong.

Author-Illustrator Contact

It is unlikely that you will have any contact whatsoever with the illustrator. This may seem harsh and detrimental to your book, but if you can learn to accept this as standard procedure, you will come to see that it most often works out for the best. If you are not an illustrator, you don't have an illustrator's eye for what works well in picture books. They seem to just know from what perspective the picture should be viewed, how to create action scenes with just the right amount of action, and how to portray characters in a way that will enhance the text, not take away from it. These people are hired for a reason and you must learn to trust their intuitions and experience.

FACT

Sometimes publishers allow the author to see the rough artwork and provide input before the art is finalized. If this happens, consider yourself lucky and don't be nitpicky with feedback or you may lose your opportunity to view unfinished art in the future.

No matter how tempted you may be to make your opinions known, you shouldn't track down your illustrator to give him your impressions or to provide instructions for your book. Anything that needs to be known should first go through your editor. The editor will decide which instructions are to be kept and see that the illustrator receives the guidance needed.

Submitting Photos

The protocol for photos is different from that of illustrations. Sometimes children's books, especially works of nonfiction, will call for photographs. In this case, it is often acceptable for the author to submit samples and suggestions along with the manuscript. This issue needs to be clarified at the beginning of the project. Obtaining photographs can be a costly and time-consuming venture. The responsibility for locating photos, clearing copyrights, and staying within the budged allocated by the publisher for the book may remain within the art department, or it may be shared by the author. In any case, this will all be negotiated early in the project.

Consider this before submitting suggestions or samples along with your manuscript. Are you willing to put forth the effort to research and gain permissions for photos? If your editor agrees that your idea is a fantastic one, a clause may be added to your contract stating that you are responsible for researching and obtaining permission to use specified photos in your book.

Technical Art

Like photographs, technical art is often an exception to the rule. If you are writing a nonfiction piece, you may need technical art to better explain what you are saying in the text. For instance, if you write a book on how to build a kite using household materials, you may want to use technical art to illustrate step-by-step instructions.

QUESTION

What is technical art?
Technical art is used to illustrate and explain specialized, mechanical, or scientific subjects based on fact. Technical art can range from diagrams to maps to instructional illustrations.

Don't worry, this doesn't mean that you need to be an accomplished artist. Often a publishing company will hire an illustrator to render the technical art based on reference material. If you believe that the inclusion of technical art will better your book, you may want to either sketch the art yourself or dig up other materials that can be used to give the artist an idea of your vision. Of course, your sketches or reference materials aren't likely to be the only thing the artist has to go on. Often the artist will also require written guidance as well as a copy of your manuscript.

Of course, it is the publisher who makes the final decision, so don't trouble yourself with finding or creating reference materials for *all* the technical art you think should be included. You will, however, want to include a few samples of what you plan to provide and outline in a cover letter exactly those sections of the text you believe would best benefit from the inclusion of technical art.

While it is possible that the editor will decide to take care of the reference material on her end, it is best to be prepared if you plan to propose its insertion. Again, you will present yourself in a professional manner if you show that you are willing to do all that you can to aid in the production of the book.

If this is a nonfiction work, you will be considered the expert on the matter and will most likely know best what art should be included. If the editor does decide to take on this task, you may be asked for your input and guidance. You may also be required to look over the rough artwork to okay its accuracy.

While you normally should not correct an illustrator's pictures in storybooks or other works of fiction if those pictures differ from your vision, you do need to correct a technical artist if the illustrations do not meet the requirements of the technical art. Keep in mind that rendering technical art is not an easy task, especially if the artist is not familiar with the subject matter. Therefore, keep your criticism polite and professional and do not be discouraged if there are several corrections that need to be made in the rough drawings. Just remember that whoever is illustrating your book is doing his or her best to create a spectacular children's book.

CHAPTER 10

Finding the Right Publisher

To give your manuscript a decent shot at success, you need to find out which publishers are interested in your type of book. Without the proper research, you may find that your manuscript is being rejected just because you sent it to the wrong publishing houses. Compiling a list of appropriate publishers takes some legwork, but it is well worth it in the end. This chapter will help you begin your search for the right publisher for your book.

Narrowing the List

Your goal is to find a publisher that will welcome your book to its list. This might be a small house or a large one; it might be one that publishes books for many different audiences or it might be one dedicated to the singular pursuit of publishing books for children. The most important thing is that the company publishes books like yours.

The best way to begin your search for the ideal publisher for your manuscript is by answering a few questions. The answers to the following questions will help you to narrow down the list of possibilities (which at this point is all publishing companies!):

- Is your book fiction or nonfiction?
- What age group is your book written for? (Is it a picture book, chapter book, etc.)
- To which market(s) will your book be sold (trade, mass-market, etc.)?
- Under what subject would your book be categorized?
- Could your book be used in classrooms—is it educational?

You should have already researched books similar to yours. Take a look at where these books are sold and where they are shelved. This should give you a further understanding of what categories your book fits into.

Creating a List of Possibilities

Once you have categorized your book, start seeking out potential publishers for it. A quick Google search of the titles from your "similar titles" list should lead to each book's publishing information. For additional help, visit a bookstore or library and jot down the names of publishing companies from the inside front covers of books in the section where you picture yours sitting. And don't forget word of mouth—talk to the people in your writers' group, or from your writing program, and see if they have any suggestions. At this point, you are almost ready to begin building your list.

Creating a list of possibilities doesn't mean that you should send your manuscript to every single one. Mergers and acquisitions are always taking place. The publishing company you may have come across during your search at a library may no longer be in existence. Or maybe the publishing company still exists but no longer publishes your type of book. You will need to conduct further research to narrow down the list of possibilities.

Organizing the Possibilities

The first step is to create a master list of publishing houses that publish children's books. Not all of these companies will be exclusively focused on children's books. For example, you will probably want to include some of the major literary houses, such as HarperCollins or Simon & Schuster, which have children's divisions, but which also publish books in other areas. The more organized you are, the easier it will be to put together a manuscript submission or query letter. You may want to create a database or spreadsheet to hold all the necessary information you will need for the potential publishers. If you aren't sure how to set up a database or spreadsheet, simple tutorials can be found online. Of course, a good old-fashioned notebook works, too!

FACT

Most publishing companies have extensive websites detailing recently published, and soon-to-be published titles. These pages can be an invaluable source of information for you, as they will show what the myriad children's book publishing companies are currently interested in.

As you conduct further research, you may find that you eliminate several of the possible publishing companies. This is a good thing: you are developing a sense of where your book fits into the market. Think of this process as cutting down on the number of rejection letters you will receive.

Gathering Information

Once you have a list of possibilities, you need to begin gathering as much information about them as you can. For each publisher on your list, you want to find out if it is an imprint, a major publishing company, or a small publishing company. You want to know: What markets does it target? Does the company specialize in children's books, or does it have only a children's division? How many titles does it publish a year? Also jot down notes or clip articles from trade publications that pertain to these companies.

QUESTION

What is an imprint?
A single publisher may publish under several different names, with each name representing a different category of books. For example, Random House publishes under the name of Bantam Books, which represents its paperback line of adult fiction and nonfiction. Bantam Books is an imprint.

You will want to pull together addresses, phone numbers, and contact names for each of these companies. The publishing company's website should contain all the necessary information, from the person to contact to titles on their current list, backlist titles, and submission guidelines. However, personnel in publishing companies changes frequently, so it is a good idea to call ahead and verify that that person still works there and has the same title.

The following sections highlight places you can look to help you get started in your research. Of course, these aren't the only resources out there. Take your time and gather as much information as you can.

Children's Writer's & Illustrator's Market

The *Children's Writer's & Illustrator's Market* is a handy reference guide to have on hand when researching publishing companies. The book is updated annually and provides listings of both book and magazine publishers specific to children's literature and a description of what they publish. The book provides contact names, e-mail addresses, websites, submission guidelines, and pay rates.

This book also includes other valuable information, such as guidelines for writing query letters and cover letters, mission statements from publishers, and articles on high-interest subjects such as contract negotiation and networking. You can find information on contests, awards, conferences, workshops, and organizations, as well as get advice from professionals in the industry.

Literary Market Place

The *Literary Market Place* (often referred to as the *LMP*) is an annual directory of American and Canadian publishers. Here you will be able to find almost anything you are searching for within the publishing industry. You will want to concentrate on its lists of publishing companies. The listings include name, address, telephone number, a description of what types of books the company publishes (young adult, general trade, textbooks, etc.), categories of books published (fiction, nonfiction, poetry, etc.), and contact names.

The *Literary Market Place* is quite expensive and you may not want to spring for the cost just yet. Fortunately, most libraries carry a copy in their reference departments—just be prepared to do a lot of copying. If you are interested in the information found in this gigantic book, you may also consider visiting *www.literarymarketplace.com*. Here you will be able to access limited information, including information on small presses and names and addresses of some publishing companies.

If you can afford it, you may subscribe to LiteraryMarketPlace.com and have access to the entire database, which includes everything in the print version. The database is easy to search and will help you to narrow down exactly what you are looking for, saving you a lot of time in the long run.

ESSENTIAL

The *Literary Market Place* also offers descriptions and contact information for editorial services companies, literary agents, wholesalers, sales representatives, and translators. You will find listings for associations, courses, events, and awards as well.

The Children's Book Council

The Children's Book Council is a nonprofit trade organization whose members include U.S. trade children's book publishers. While you can't become a member, you do have access to its list of members. The list includes the publishing company's name, address, phone number, type and format of the books it publishes, and general submission guidelines. You will also be provided with contact names, though you will need to double check them. You can get this list in either hard copy or by visiting the Children's Book Council's website. If you view the list from the Internet, you will also see links to the publishers' websites.

Keep in mind that although this list provides a great deal of information, it is not complete. It lists only those companies that are members of the Children's Book Council. You will want to continue your research through other sources.

For more information about the Children's Book Council, visit its website at *www.cbcbooks.org*; write to The Children's Book Council, 12 West 37th Street, 2nd Floor, New York, NY 10018; or call 212-966-1990.

Asking Around

While publications are great for gathering facts, sometimes you want more than just the facts. This is where social networking comes in. Talk to anyone and everyone you know who may be able to help you in your search for the perfect publisher. This includes anyone who is directly involved in children's publishing (such as an editor or sales representative), book buyers for bookstores, children's librarians, other writers, or literary agents. Remember that any information you gather, no matter how trivial it may seem, may be put to use later on.

Inside Scoop

Do you know anyone who currently works in the book publishing industry? Contact her and bring along your list of potential publishers. See if she can offer any inside information. Maybe you don't personally know anyone in the industry, but maybe you know someone who knows someone with answers. Here's where online social media can help you. Put the word out on Twitter, Facebook, and LinkedIn that you are preparing to send your manuscript to publishers. By simply making your presence and your project known, you can begin to create a public relations (PR) platform (something all writers need these days), and broaden your scope of industry connections.

Whether or not you are able to directly link to anyone in the children's book publishing industry, you can certainly use social media to gain an insider's perspective. Once you have the names of a few editors at the publishing companies on your list, you can begin following those people on Twitter. This will give you a clearer sense of where their attentions lie, and may even help you decide how to frame your query.

You may discover that a certain publishing company is looking to produce a new series, though this news has not been made public. If your manuscript has series potential, you may want to include that in your cover letter, giving you a bit of an edge over other writers. Following industry insiders through social media outlets could lead you to find out about an emerging publishing company likely to embrace your type of book, or an already established company looking to expand its children's department.

You may discover that your manuscript will not fit in with a particular publisher's list as you thought it would. Or maybe a publisher is working on a manuscript that is very similar to yours and probably would not include two such similar titles on its list. Knowing where your book won't fit is as important as knowing where it will—and who knows? Maybe your next book will be perfect for your original choice. The important thing is that now you have the knowledge to make educated decisions about where to send your manuscript.

Guidelines from the Publishers

Once you have a list of publishers, check each one's website for writer's guidelines. Each will have its own list. The first thing you need to know is whether or not the company is currently accepting unsolicited manuscripts. Unsolicited manuscripts are those that are not specifically requested by an editor or publisher. Your manuscript will most likely be unsolicited material.

If the guidelines state that the company does not accept unsolicited manuscripts, don't try to send it in anyway. Doing so tells an editor that you either haven't bothered to check out the guidelines or, even worse, have read the guidelines but decided to ignore them. Even if you are certain your manuscript would be a good match for the company's line of books, you can't force yourself on an editor. It is likely that your manuscript will not even be looked at, so don't waste the time, energy, and expense.

If the company does accept unsolicited manuscripts, you need to present your work in a professional manner. Following the guidelines on the website to a T shows the editor you have done your homework and have respect for the company's protocol. If you are confident that your manuscript is right for a particular publisher, take the time to format your submission according to the company's exact specifications. This will give you a leg up on the writers who send in their manuscripts without regard for the publisher's requirements, and will help gain your project the attention you seek from an editor.

Subsidy Publishers

As you are researching publishing companies, you may come across advertisements from companies promising to publish your book. Finally! Someone understands the hardships writers face in trying to reach the shelves and has taken steps to make it easy, right? Don't be fooled by these advertisements. There is no easy way to get your book published, distributed to the proper markets, and into the hands of children. If becoming successful within children's publishing was so easy, everyone would be full-time children's writers.

ESSENTIAL

Even if your manuscript has been declined by all the potential publishers on your list, it may just be that your manuscript isn't quite ready for publication. If an editor doesn't feel as though she can sell your book, how are *you* going to?

Have you ever heard the expression "too good to be true"? These advertisements are just that. Normally, the companies behind the ads are subsidy publishers, AKA vanity presses. Subsidy publishers can indeed publish your book, but the catch is that you pay for it. You pay a fee (sometimes an exorbitant sum) and the subsidy publisher will turn your manuscript into a set number of books and deliver them to your doorstep. If you are confident that your manuscript is top-quality children's literature but you can't get it published, you may find subsidy publishing tempting. You might reach a point where you are unable to find a publisher that is a good match for your book, or where your manuscript has been rejected by all potential publishers on your list, and you are searching for new ways to make a splash with your book. Here comes a company offering to publish the book, no questions asked.

Unfortunately, subsidy publishers won't get you very far in the publishing world. They do publish your book, but the rest is up to you. Most likely you will have to market your book. You will have to raise awareness of yourself and of your book. You will have to take time to convince booksellers that your book is worth stocking on their shelves. You will essentially have to become a publisher.

If you find yourself at a dead end and leaning toward subsidy publishing, put your manuscript through another revision process or two. Do further research into publishing companies. Try to find another angle from which to pitch your manuscript. Or consider hiring a professional editor to help you take your book to the next level, and then try sending it out again. Remember: writing is an endurance game.

Self-Publishing

Some people resist the temptation of subsidy publishers, and instead turn to the idea of self-publishing. You know that your book is worth publishing, so why not do it yourself? This way you don't have to bother researching publishing companies, abiding by writer's guidelines, convincing editors of your manuscript's worth, and facing rejection. Plus you get to design your own cover, illustrate the book however you please, charge whatever you want, and reap all the profits. The only problem is that you have to work very hard and know precisely what you're doing to make a profit.

A publishing company does a lot more than just accept and reject manuscripts and send them off to the printer. You will have to learn the business in full if you wish to be successful with self-publishing. If you thought locating publishing companies was a lot of work, you may not want to dive headfirst into one-person publishing. One of the largest considerations for anyone thinking about self-publishing is the cost. You need to have the capital to get started. You can't make money without spending money in self-publishing.

Caution! Wide Workload

Self-publishing requires that you take on the roles of several people. You will have to be the writer, the editor, the publisher, the art director, the designer, the sales rep, the publicist, and the accountant. Your book will need to go through the same process as those in traditional publishing. If you try to take shortcuts, they will show up in the quality of the book. Therefore you may need to hire a copyeditor, proofreader, illustrator, and printer.

While the idea of planning and executing a book by yourself from start to finish may sound like a fun challenge, there are a vast number of decisions to be made, many of which require professional skill. Will the book be hardcover or paperback? What will be the trim size? What will be the price? Will you have color or black-and-white illustrations? Who will do the illustrations? How will you market your book? How many books will you initially print? What type of paper will you use? You must also decide on printing and binding companies.

You will have to design not only front and back covers but also the interior. If you include illustrations, you will have to learn about art reproduction. You will have to assign an ISBN. If you want the public to purchase your book, you will have to find a way to get it into stores. Distributors, who place books for publishing companies, will be wary of working with a previously unpublished author, so you may have to do this part yourself as well.

QUESTION

What is an ISBN?
ISBN stands for International Standard Book Number. This is a number on the copyright page and the back cover of a book, usually close to the bar code. This number gives a book its identity and assists order fulfillment and inventory.

Self-publishing requires huge commitment, and involves huge financial risk. Research all the particulars of self-publishing before making any decisions, and before investing any money.

When Self-Publishing Works

Under the right circumstances, self-publishing can be successful. If you have a deep knowledge of the publishing business (including online marketing) or a significant following of potential customers for your book, self-publishing can be a good option. Let's say you are a doctor with your own popular radio program and a website dedicated to the subject of your book. You have the audience and expertise needed to market your book, and you have access to thousands of listeners every week. If you hire the right people to design and produce your book, self-publishing could be the most lucrative way to go—after all, you would be earning all of the profits from book sales, and you could easily promote the project through your clients and listeners.

Even those without a built-in media base have the power to create a platform and make self-publishing work for them—but it takes serious time, knowledge, and money.

While it is recommended that you first try to get published through traditional publishing houses, if you are determined to self-publish your work then there are several reference guides available to you, such as *The Self-Publishing Manual* by Dan Poynter. You may also considering hiring a consultant to give you advice and show you the ropes so you don't feel as though you are *completely* on your own.

CHAPTER 11

Considering an Agent

Do you really need an agent? That question is for you to answer, but this chapter will offer all the information you need to make an educated decision. What exactly does a book agent do? How do you find one, and how do you know if the one you found is legit? You may wonder why writers are always thanking their agents in the front of their books and in interviews. Can't a writer do it all herself? Here's the inside scoop.

An Agent's Job

A literary agent works as a go-between for writers and publishers. This includes sending the manuscript to editors, negotiating contracts, and handling payments and royalty statements. Both aspiring and seasoned writers can benefit greatly from the assistance of a good agent. If an agent is on board with your project, he will take quite a load of responsibility from you and can get your manuscript into the hands of editors you otherwise would not have had the means to reach.

It is an agent's job to know how to negotiate the publishing industry. Agents are up-to-date on current market information; they know what books are currently being published, what trends have passed, and how to frame a book idea in marketing terms. They know what publishers are looking for. They know who to contact and have established relationships with editors at large and small publishing houses. Bottom line: it is an agent's job to represent you and convince editors to publish your work, and they have the unique experience to do so.

ESSENTIAL

You can trust that a good agent is going to help you get the best deal possible for your manuscript. Having an agent on your side will relieve you of the stress of having to learn how to negotiate a contract. (However, it is always a good idea for you to learn about contracts, so you feel confident about what you are signing.) An agent will know what the going rate is for your type of book, as well as what the typical contract stipulations are.

Opening Doors

Some publishing companies do not accept unsolicited manuscripts. On your own, you would not be able to get the attention of an editor working for one of these houses. An agent can. Agented manuscripts find their way directly into the hands of editors who are best able to give them consideration; without an agent, your manuscript may spend months waiting for the attention it deserves.

Unsolicited manuscripts go into the "slush pile," which an editorial assistant is tasked with wading through. Keep in mind that a high number of those manuscripts will either be inappropriate for that particular publisher or just flat-out terrible. Having yours mixed in with all the others doesn't always bode well. For one, you are relying on the opinion of an editorial assistant, or an unpaid intern, for your manuscript to even reach the desk of an editor. Secondly, you could be waiting several months for your manuscript to go through the needed channels, all the while wondering if you should wait for this particular publisher to respond or should go ahead and send your manuscript elsewhere.

ALERT

Agents do not take all potential clients under their wings. Quite often, agents already have an extensive client list that they must address before taking on anything else. Although they may want to, some simply do not have the time or energy to devote to editing or delivering book concepts.

Agents can get your manuscript in the door and on the desk of an editor quickly. Agents also know just the right buttons to push with editors. It is their job to *sell* your manuscript. Therefore, they know what phrases and statistics to use; they know what aspects of the manuscript should be addressed; and they know how to build excitement and enthusiasm. In addition to being book lovers, they are experts in the art of the sales pitch.

Help Along the Way

When an agent believes in a client, or in a particular book project, he may be willing to spend a great deal of time working with the writer to turn an idea into something that can sell. Many agents edit book proposals by hand—many even suggest what books their clients should write. Whereas a publishing company may simply send you a rejection letter without explaining exactly why the manuscript was unsuitable, an agent may decline the manuscript as is, but recognize the promise in your abilities and work with you to create a publishable manuscript. Agents are in the business of building writers' careers. After all, if a writer becomes successful, her agent also becomes successful.

Hands-on technique varies from agent to agent. Depending on the size of the agent's client list, or the busyness of a particular season, some agents will edit your manuscript, while others may recommend hiring a freelance editor and provide you with contact names. Others will briefly state in a letter what you need to work on or what they would like to see done to the manuscript.

The Tradeoff

Agents do a tremendous amount of skillful work on behalf of their clients, so naturally they need to be compensated. Agents help their writers shape manuscripts and secure contracts with major publishers. If you want an agent to do these things for you, understand that the two things you must give to your agent are money and control.

Money

The good news is the publisher will pay the agent. The bad news is that it is your money the agent is taking a cut from. Because agents handle the monies and royalty statements, the check cut for your manuscript is sent to your agent. The agent takes out a commission between 10 and 20 percent (usually 15 for domestic sales), and then cuts a check to you for the remaining money.

Sometimes agents working for small agencies or operating their own businesses also expect to be reimbursed for certain expenses. Most often these expenses will include such things as postage, express deliveries, photocopies, and so on. These expenses will range from about $150 to $300 initially, and could be charged up front. Beware of any agent charging you much more than $300 in up-front overhead fees. Be sure to ask if there are any additional expenses that you will be required to incur. Also keep in mind that these expenses should not be charged to you without your permission; anything deducted from your check should have been approved by you beforehand.

You will almost always have to sign a contract with the agent. The contract should cover the agent's compensation, how long the contract remains in effect, and exactly what the agent is responsible for.

Control

While having an agent take on the responsibility of submission certainly makes your job easier, it's important to understand that by taking on an agent you have to give up a level of control. Trust that the agent is going to do his job to the best of his abilities. It is the agent's job to place your manuscript. If you don't feel comfortable leaving the selling to someone else, then don't hire an agent.

If you have specific publishing companies in mind that you believe would be a good fit for your book, the most you can do is pass the names along to your agent. It is unlikely that you will have direct control over the submission process. While a good agent will consider your suggestions, especially if you can back them up with reasons why your manuscript would fit the company's list, the agent doesn't have to act on them. An agent's priority is to sell your manuscript, and your thoughts on a particular publisher may not be in line with your agent's more experienced view. In this case, you have to trust your agent's knowledge of the industry.

FACT

A lot of trust is involved (on both sides) in taking on an agent. It is important that before you sign a contract with an agency, you know that the agent is someone you can work well with. You are attempting to create a lasting professional relationship, one that will lead to several book contracts and an overall boost in your career.

Also keep in mind that responses from editors will go through your agent. You may not even see them at all. You will also have to hand over control of contract negotiations. You can bet that your agent will do his best to get you a good deal, since he gets paid a percentage of your negotiated fee. You always have final authority over whether or not to sign the contract, but negotiating the best deal possible is the sole job of your agent.

Where to Look

So you want an agent, but you aren't sure where to find one. There are several good places to search for suitable agents, but finding a good agent can be trickier than finding a publisher, and finding the right one for you may take a fair amount of time and energy. If your primary motive for finding an agent is to avoid all the research you would have to do to find a publisher, you may be disappointed. There is no quick and easy approach to getting your book published, although once you find the right agent, you can stop focusing on how to get published and get back to writing. There are quite a few places you can search for an agent, some more reliable than others. Start with those listed here, but don't limit your search to only these.

Association of Authors' Representatives

The Association of Authors' Representatives (AAR) is an excellent resource for finding legitimate literary agents. The AAR has a strict canon of ethics that agents must adhere to in order to be members. For instance, to qualify for membership, the agent must have been practicing for at least two years and can't charge the client up-front fees.

You can find the list of members, which includes names and addresses, by visiting *www.aar-online.org*. You will also find here AAR's membership qualifications and Canon of Ethics.

Literary Market Place

The *Literary Market Place* (*LMP*), mentioned in Chapter 10 as a top resource for finding a publisher, can also help you find an agent. The *LMP* includes a section devoted to literary agents, including international agents. Here you will find names, addresses, and specialties included in the profiles, among other information.

ESSENTIAL

While those listed in the *LMP* are required to provide at least three letters of recommendation, you should still conduct your own background research before signing on with an agent. You can never be too careful with the manuscript you worked so hard to produce.

Writer's Digest Guide to Literary Agents

The *Writer's Digest Guide to Literary Agents* is a handy guide for the author determined to secure the representation of an agent. Here you will find the necessary contact information for over 500 literary agencies. You will also find submission guidelines and individual needs specific to each of these agencies.

AgentQuery.com

AgentQuery.com is a website dedicated to helping writers find legitimate representation. This site is easy to use and is constantly being updated. Search results include the name of the agent, the name of the agency, the postal address, the web address, the genres represented, and whether or not they are currently accepting queries. All the agents in their database have been thoroughly screened, and the service is free for writers.

Agent Research & Evaluation

Agent Research & Evaluation (AR&E) is a company that provides a number of services to help you locate an agent. This is a business and they charge fees (ranging from $25 to $240) for most of their services. They conduct the research on agents and provide you with a detailed report of the agent's deals. If you can justify the cost, this can be a very valuable source of information for your research needs.

AR&E also provides a free service through which you give the company an agent's name and it will tell you whether there is a public record on that particular agent and/or if there are any negative reports about him or her. You can also find a list of agents, though only names are provided. Visit *www.agentresearch.com* or write to Agent Research & Evaluation, 334 East 30th Street, New York, NY 10014 for more information.

Researching Your Agent

It is imperative that you know your agent before conducting any type of business with her. You want to know that your manuscript will be properly represented. Good literary agents can work wonders in their fields of specialty.

A not-so-good literary agent can alienate prospective editors for your work and reduce your chances of getting published.

Unfortunately, there are a lot of scam artists out there who prey on the eagerness (or desperation) of first-time writers. Don't let your enthusiasm get the better of your judgment.

Pre-Contact Research

While your initial search will likely provide a long list of names, not all of these will be suitable for your type of manuscript. Sending a query letter to an agent who does not handle your type of book will be a waste of time for both you and the agent. Check the websites of all the agents on your list, and only query those definitely handling children's books like yours. If your book is a board book for toddlers, don't send your query to an agent whose only children's book clients are those writing teen mysteries.

ALERT

Keep an eye out for two good warning signs that will flag scam artists: literary agents who charge you fees before selling your manuscript (though some will require that you pay for certain expenses such as mailing) and literary agents who seek you out (unless, of course, you are a big-name author).

Pre-Signing Research

Let's jump ahead a bit and say that you have an agent interested in representing you. While you may be overjoyed and certain that all your dreams are about to come true, you need to settle yourself down and take a rational approach. Do not immediately sign a contract with the agency. You need to find out a few things first:

- Is the agent a member of the Association of Authors' Representatives?
- How long has the agent been practicing?
- How long has she dealt with children's books?
- Discuss the agent's compensation. Will any additional fees be charged to your account?

- Find out how involved you will be in the submission process. Will the agent notify you of all submissions and offers?
- What children's books has the agent sold? Has she sold many books recently?
- To what publishing companies has the agent sold books?
- Ask the agent to provide a list of references.

Of course, many of these questions can be answered by carefully reading through the agent's website, but be sure to verify any facts listed. After reviewing the website, make a list of questions that haven't been answered. Use the above list, but also add other questions you may have. The AAR's website, *www.aar-online.org*, also provides a list of questions to ask an agent.

When talking to a prospective agent, pay attention to how she listens and responds to your questions. Is this the kind of person you would want to do business with? Be cautious and go with your gut instinct.

ESSENTIAL

If it is at all possible to meet the agent in person, do. Having the opportunity to discuss things face-to-face will give you a better sense of how she will handle the care and sale of your manuscript.

Feel free to ask the agent to clarify anything you don't understand. If the agent is vague or unwilling to answer your questions, don't sign on with her. It's a good bet she will be equally vague throughout your working relationship. Even if the agent is legitimate, you shouldn't be left in the dark when it comes to understanding the process of getting your book sold.

Submitting to an Agent

First of all, you need to have a completed manuscript before you consider getting an agent. An agent won't represent you based solely on your ideas, especially if you have not been previously published. Make sure your manuscript has gone through the needed revision process however many times it takes to get it as close to perfect as you can. You must be confident in your work if you want it to go any farther than your own desk.

The Query Letter

While each agency has its own submission guidelines, most often agents ask to only be sent a query letter at first. The query letter is your introduction. You should keep it very short and to the point. Don't let your letter go beyond a page. Put your writing skills to the test here.

You should introduce yourself and state that you are interested in finding representation for your book. Mention any works you have previously published. (Agents are more likely to take on writers who have already proven their abilities and have their work out there.) If you haven't been published, don't apologize or make excuses, just don't address this issue.

If you have any credentials that will help sell the book, mention these. Maybe you have a popular blog or kids' website, or maybe you give presentations on the same subject as your book—anything that shows you have an audience can help your case.

ESSENTIAL

Keep in mind that the query letter is your initial contact. You will have to write a strong letter to capture the agent's attention and get her excited about the book—and you. If you manage this, the agent will then ask to see your manuscript. From there, your manuscript will be your primary selling tool.

State what type of book you have written (middle-grade historical fiction, fiction picture book, young adult novel, etc.) and give a brief description. Keep it short! Just write one or two paragraphs describing the book in a fun, intriguing way. Remember, your goal at this point is just to develop enough interest in your idea that the agent asks you to send your manuscript.

Proofread your letter, make sure your contact information is clear, and send it off, making sure to enclose a self-addressed stamped envelope for a response. You will probably want to send queries to several agents at once. There aren't any rules pertaining to this, but keep in mind that for an unpublished author, the odds are against you in finding an agent. Therefore, it may be best to send query letters in batches of, say, ten to save time. Don't be discouraged if your first batch comes back without an invitation to send in your completed manuscript; just go to the next ten on your list and keep your fingers crossed.

Manuscript Submission

If an agent asks to see your manuscript or a sample, send it right away. You've already captured the agent's interest; don't give him time to forget you. Agents deal with many query letters every day, and until you are signed, you aren't the agent's main priority. Also be sure to follow the agent's instructions—don't send in a completed manuscript if the agent wants to see only a chapter.

Read over your manuscript one more time before submitting it. Watch for typos and make sure you haven't left in any notes to yourself. The submission should look clean and professional.

The Final Decision

Rather than flat-out rejecting your work, several agents may request to see your full manuscript. This is a very good sign, but it does not guarantee an offer of representation. You will probably be declined more than once at this stage in the process. Once an agent does come forward with an offer, the final decision to sign with him is, of course, yours to make. Take some time to think this through before diving in headfirst. You will have to do a lot of work either way—whether you decide to find an agent or submit to publishing companies yourself.

The Pros and Cons

On one hand, an agent who has agreed to represent you is confident in his ability to sell your manuscript. He already knows whom to contact and how to pitch your manuscript. He has experience and expertise that you don't. He will be a big help in taking you through your first publication. He will be able to open doors that you couldn't open on your own. He will make sure you get a good deal and work with you to publish even more. A lot can be said for having a good agent on your side.

On the other hand, you don't necessarily need an agent to get published. While there are certainly several publishers of adult literature that do not accept unsolicited or unagented material, the children's publishing industry is slightly more accepting of unsolicited material. You will need to know the market and the various publishers anyway, so perhaps the main factor will not be your time and energy, but rather the level of your sales and contract expertise.

Money is another big thing to consider. An agent will take 10 to 20 percent of what you make. This can add up to a lot, when you could potentially do the work yourself and keep all the profits. Plus, it can be just as hard for an unpublished author to find an agent as it is to find a publisher—in which case, the time you put into finding an agent could have been used to find a publisher.

When the Time Is Right

You also have the option of contacting publishers and pitching your manuscript yourself, then getting an agent when you reach the contract stage. This will give you complete control over your manuscript and the submission process and gain you the support of an ally who will go to bat for you. Agents know the legal jargon associated with publishing contracts. They know how to negotiate with the publishers. And they know what type of deal to expect. Many authors find contract negotiation to be a little tricky, especially if they are first-time writers.

FACT

If you don't want to pay an agent's commission on a book you sold yourself, you may want to consider hiring a lawyer for a one-time fee to go over the contract for you. Many lawyers will not have dealt with publishing contracts, so you should try to find one who has.

You shouldn't have a problem getting an agent if you have already reached the contract stage. This is easy money for a literary agent. You may wonder why you would need an agent at this stage if you have already done the rest of the work yourself. Well, you don't really *need* an agent, but it is good to have one. And as long as you are under contract with an agent, he will help sell your next books, making this whole process more straightforward in the future.

CHAPTER 12

Submitting a Manuscript

Reaching the submission stage is a very exciting time. You have worked very hard to write and revise, and have developed a list of publishers that might provide a good home for your book. Now you need to bring the two together. This chapter will help you do just that.

Preparing the Manuscript

Preparing the manuscript for submission is not difficult, but it is important. Basically, you just want the manuscript to look clean and professional. Make sure it is typed in a double-spaced standard font, such as Times New Roman or Courier, with one-inch margins on all sides. Also, make sure the color is black, and the font size is 12. Keep italics and bold to a minimum and use them only if absolutely necessary. Nothing should distract readers from the content of your story, so keep the format plain and simple.

Add consecutive page numbers either at the bottom or top right-hand corner of the page. Do not start a new sequence with new chapters; continue the numbering all the way through, as in a published book.

Print the manuscript on white paper; refrain from using bright colors to bring attention to your manuscript. The paper should be good quality, not the flimsy computer paper that is easily torn. Your manuscript will likely pass through several hands and you don't want the final (and probably most important!) person to miss sections or have difficulty reading it.

Last, but not least, make a copy of your manuscript, formatted exactly like the one you are sending off. Email the copy to yourself as an attachment. This will protect you against hard drive crashes.

Picture Book and Early Reader Layout

If you are submitting a picture book or early reader, present the text as if it were a continuous short story. In other words, don't display a single line per page. Most of the time, editors will determine where to insert page breaks. Occasionally, you may have a strong opinion about the location of a break. In this case, simply hit return on your keyboard, and leave one blank line in your text.

ALERT

Do not turn a page over or upside down in the middle of your manuscript in a sneaky attempt to see if an editor has read it all the way through. This trick tends to alienate editors since they know what you're doing. Plus, this isn't a very professional way to conduct yourself; you might as well sign your cover letter "Amateur."

Place your name, address, and telephone number in the upper left-hand corner of the first page, single-spaced. In the upper right-hand corner, type the approximate word count. Most word processing programs will tell you what your word count is. Microsoft Word shows you the word count at the bottom of the page. Center your story's working title about one-third of the way down the page. Skip a couple of lines and begin your story. Because these books normally do not have a lot of text, it wouldn't look right to have a separate title page.

Chapter, Middle-Grade, and Young Adult Books

If you are submitting a chapter, middle-grade, or young adult book, you should follow the basic guidelines from the previous section unless the publisher has its own specific guidelines. However, you may also want to add a title page to make your submission look more attractive. Just as you would do with picture books and early readers, place your name, address, and telephone number in the upper left-hand corner of the title page, single-spaced. Place the approximate word count in the upper right-hand corner. Type your working title in all caps almost halfway down the page. Type your byline just a couple of lines beneath the title—this could be your real name or pen name, whatever you want to be published under.

On the next page, begin your story. Center the chapter title down a couple of lines from the top, and begin your text a couple of lines beneath that. Always double space your text. For each new chapter, start a new page. Number your manuscript pages beginning with the first page of the first chapter; do not number the title page. Again, number the pages consecutively, from the first page of the book to the last. Some publishers may require that the author's last name appear at the top of every page; check the publishers' guidelines for these specifics.

Package Appearance

You will want to create a submission packet with the appearance of professionalism and quality. Do not bind your manuscript using staples, a three-ring binder, glue, or string. Editors prefer to have unbound submissions, fastened only with a large clip.

Now that you have your manuscript ready to go, you are almost there. You also need to include a cover letter and a self-addressed stamped envelope (SASE) (we will discuss these later in the chapter).

FACT

Some writers enclose a self-addressed stamped postcard and ask the editor to return it when she receives the manuscript. While this may sound like a good idea, it can actually cause a great amount of frustration on your part. Not all editors will return this card, even though they have received the manuscript. Look in the submission guidelines to see if there is mention of a confirmation postcard.

If your packet is just a few pages long, as most picture book and early reader submissions are, you can use a regular business-size envelope for the submission. Anything more than a few pages long should be sent in a standard manila envelope. You can either print out address labels or handwrite the mailing address very neatly. Don't bother sending the packet express delivery. You will have to wait quite a while to get a response anyway, so there's no point in spending the extra money. Just send it first class through the U.S. mail.

Submission Guidelines

Always, always, always follow submission guidelines specific to individual publishing companies! You should have this information already, having thoroughly researched the publishing companies on your list. However, if for some reason you don't have this information, get it now. It may feel like the different publishing companies are making you jump through hoops by requiring different formatting, but this is one easy way for them to weed out manuscripts. People who don't take the time to read the publisher's rules are clearly not serious about finding a home for their book.

While some publishing companies accept unsolicited manuscripts, many of the large ones accept agented submissions only

It is unlikely that "we accept unsolicited manuscripts" will be the extent of a publishing company's submission guidelines. Often you will find other requirements concerning issues such as multiple submissions (discussed later in this chapter), sample material versus full manuscript, query letters, mailing address, envelopes, formatting and layout, illustrations, and confirmation postcards. Of course, the requirements vary from publisher to publisher, so some may cover more issues than those we've mentioned, while others may not cover any.

Guideline Do's

There are several things submission guidelines will tell you to do. For example, let's say you have found a publishing company's submission guidelines posted on its website. This company does accept unsolicited manuscripts, but it has separate guidelines for different categories of books. You read through the categories and determine that your picture book fits in with the company's needs. You skip to the page or paragraph that gives you the guidelines for this category.

The guidelines specify that you should send in a completed picture book text, along with a cover letter; a query letter is not needed. You are told to submit it on 8½" × 11" plain white paper, unbound. The manuscript should be typed and double-spaced. Include your name, address, and telephone number on both the cover letter and the manuscript itself.

ESSENTIAL

While you can probably gather submission guidelines from already compiled lists of publishers such as the Children's Book Council's list of members, you should also visit each individual publisher's website for updated guidelines.

The guidelines may also tell you to include a self-addressed, stamped envelope (SASE) with your submission. You can either include the postage required to mail the entire manuscript (otherwise it will be thrown out), or you can include a single first class stamp on a return envelope. In the latter case, you may want to state clearly in your cover letter that your SASE is for "reply only, please recycle the manuscript." These days, with electronic files and e-mail, requesting a reply only is perfectly normal. Of course, if you prefer to retain the full manuscript, you may.

Many publishing companies have guidelines similar to these. As you can see, it isn't so difficult to follow the guideline do's.

Guideline Don'ts

Sometimes publishers also include guideline don'ts, and these should be followed just as stringently as the do's. For example, you may learn that this publishing company does want to see completed picture book text, but does not want you to send in illustrations to accompany it. (Illustrations will likely have their own set of submission guidelines outlined elsewhere on its website.)

You may also learn that this publisher does not want you to send the manuscript via e-mail or fax. Further, they do not want bound books or manuscripts laid out in book form. You may also be instructed not to include a confirmation postcard, as these are often lost in the shuffle.

While these are just an example of guideline don'ts, they should give you a good idea of what to expect from a publishing company's guidelines. Remember to follow the guidelines to a T. Any negligence on your part could result in your manuscript being returned with a rejection letter.

The Cover Letter

The cover letter is very important to your submission packet. The cover letter is what the editor will read first and can determine whether the editor actually reads the manuscript or simply returns it with a polite rejection letter. Like the manuscript, your cover letter should have a clean and professional appearance. Keep in mind that you must make a good first impression.

ESSENTIAL

Be sure to watch your spelling and grammar in the cover letter. This is the editor's first introduction to you. The last thing you want to convey is that you are a poor writer. Proofread it yourself and then have someone else proofread it for you.

Elements of a Cover Letter

The cover letter should be formatted and typed like a standard business letter. If you have letterhead, use it. If not, start the letter with your name and address, followed by the date and the publisher's name and address. Beneath this should be your salutation and then the body of the letter. Finally, add the closing, leaving room to write your signature above your typed name. Some also add an "Enclosures:" note at the bottom telling what is enclosed.

The body of the letter is very important. You want to keep it brief and to the point. Do not go beyond three paragraphs. State that you are enclosing your manuscript and give the working title. Give a brief description of your book without going into much detail. You want to entice the editor to read the book, not give a full summary.

Include relevant background information about yourself such as any published works, credentials, or expertise on the topic you have written about. If you have none of these, certainly do not announce it or apologize for it. Instead, you may choose to include a personal experience or reason why you wrote the book.

ALERT

Do not include a resume or any cutesy gimmicks with your manuscript. Resist the temptation to include your life history, sad stories that stir sympathy, or "joking" threats ("Publish my book or you'll be sorry!").

You may also include a statement regarding how your book would fit in well with the publisher's list. It is always a good idea to include something that shows you have done your homework and are familiar with the company's book list.

You should never state that your family and friends—or neighbor, mail carrier, hair stylist—thought that this was the best book ever written. Stay away from judging your own book. Obviously you believe it is quality stuff or you wouldn't have sent it. Allow the editor to make up her own mind.

What's in a Name?

If, during the course of your research, you have located the name of a specific editor, and you have double checked that she still holds the same title, then go ahead and address your query letter to her. This shows that you have put special care into researching the company, and are not sending blanket query letters to all publishing houses. However, writing to a specific editor is certainly not required. So if you don't have a name, don't sweat it.

It is quite acceptable to address the package to "Editorial Department" or "Submissions Editor." Often the submission guidelines given by publishing companies will ask you to mail your submission to a generic title or simply a department.

Query Letters and Proposals

If you have written a nonfiction work, chances are publishers' submission guidelines will request that you send in a query letter or proposal before the editor will agree to read the full-length manuscript. If an editor is not intrigued by your query letter or proposal, he will not ask to see your manuscript. However, keep in mind that even if an editor does ask to see the full manuscript, this does not mean you have sold a book—it means you've passed the first test.

Query Letters

Basically, a query letter is a letter asking an editor if he would be interested in seeing your work. Sounds easy enough. However, some writers find this to be the most difficult phase of the entire publishing process. Considering that this letter is your one shot at getting your foot in the door, you can see why it can be a little nerve-racking.

A query letter, like a cover letter, should be set up as a standard business letter. Place your name and address at the top, followed by the date and then the publisher's name and address. Open the letter with an appropriate salutation. "Dear Editor" will work just fine if you do not have a contact name. Following the closing, sign your name and print your name beneath the signature.

The body of the letter should make the editor want to read your manuscript. While this is certainly a sales pitch, avoid making extravagant claims. State the working title and what type of book you have written. Give a brief, but intriguing, description of the book. You also should provide market research and explain how your book will stand out from those currently available on the same topic. If you can give a reason why your book would fit in well with the particular publisher's list, add this too.

FACT

If your query letter has done the trick, an editor will ask to see either the full-length manuscript or a proposal. So even if the publisher's guidelines do not ask for proposals, it is usually a good idea to have a proposal on hand just in case—especially for nonfiction.

In today's publishing world, selling the author can be just as important as selling the story—this is especially the case in adult nonfiction books, but it can play an important role in children's book publishing as well.

Provide relevant background information about yourself, such as why you are qualified to write this book and whether you have published other books like it. This information helps an enthusiastic editor sell your book proposal to her company's board of directors who must give the final go-ahead. If you have any credentials or expertise in the book's specific subject matter, certainly mention them as well. For example, if you have written a book about chicken pox and you are a doctor, let the editor know. If you are the author of other books on topics similar to that of the current book, also let the editor know. If you have none of the above, a human interest story or personal experience always works well to add some flavor.

Proposals

Proposals are what fall between a full-length manuscript submission and a query letter. Normally, proposals are requested for works of nonfiction. While writers have been known to sell books on the proposal alone, it's best that you have a completed manuscript before submitting a proposal, especially as a first-time writer.

A proposal includes sample chapters of your manuscript, a cover letter, a detailed chapter-by-chapter outline, a marketing plan, and a self-addressed stamped envelope. The cover letter should be very similar to a cover letter submitted with a full-length manuscript. Again, keep it brief and professional. In fact, it should be an automatic response in sending anything to a publisher.

You will also need to provide an outline of your entire manuscript. Normally, this is somewhat similar to a table of contents. Divide your outline into chapters and then either give a brief description or list the topics that will be discussed for each chapter—if your work is nonfiction. (If you are submitting a proposal for a novel, then your outline should be replaced by a book synopsis. Think of the brief summary or blurb on the back of a soft cover book. It tells you what the book is about, and makes you want to read it. A synopsis is like an extended blurb. This is hard to write and deserves your best effort. How long should it be? A brief one will be one to ten pages; a longer one will be about one page for every 25 pages of the novel's text. Use your chapter summaries for reference, and tell the story of your book. Include bits of dialogue. Make it spirited and enticing. The synopsis must compel your reader to take a look at your sample chapters.

Next, you need to include a marketing plan. This includes market research on books like yours that have been published recently and have done well. Check the publishers' websites for recent titles—also check recent Newbery and Caldecott award winners, and any children's books featured in *Publishers Weekly*. You have to be able to convince editors that your book fits into the current market, but that it is not too similar to what is already out there. If this sounds tricky, it is. Basically, if you are turning in a nonfiction book proposal, you need to show that there is an eager market for your type of book (your subject matter and style) but that the market is not being satisfied by what is out there now. This section also shows editors that you are serious and have taken the time to find out what is going on in the book industry.

A proposal also includes sample chapters from your work. Check the publisher's submission guidelines for specifications. This gives you the opportunity to back up your fantastic book idea with a demonstration of your writing skills. Make sure the chapters you submit are your best work, well-edited.

Multiple Submissions

You have your list of potential publishers, you know what their guidelines are, and you have prepared your manuscript for submission. You are all ready to go, but should you send your manuscript to all of the publishers on your list at the same time? This is a common question for first-time writers. Unfortunately there isn't a straightforward answer.

ALERT

While you may choose to send multiple submissions, you should never create a one-size-fits-all form letter. You need to make your cover letter specific to the company you are sending it to. Also, keep in mind that different publishing companies have different submission guidelines, so it wouldn't be wise to create one submission packet that you photocopy over and over to send to all publishers.

As you will see, editors and writers have differing views on multiple submissions. Sometimes publishers will state in their submission guidelines that they want an exclusive submission or that multiple submissions are fine. But this isn't always the case, so it essentially boils down to what you are comfortable with.

The Editor's Side

While most editors are becoming more tolerant of multiple submissions because they understand the strenuous process writers are put through, some still want exclusive submissions. They want to know that the writer has taken the time to consider different publishers and has chosen to send them the manuscript first. This forces the writer to make the difficult decision of where to submit a manuscript, thus weeding out those who haven't done their homework.

You must also consider that editors are weighed down with a very heavy workload. It is sometimes difficult for them to keep their heads above water, and they can't always get to your manuscript right away. When it arrives, your manuscript must first meet the standards of a reader who will pass it along to an editor if she believes it is worthwhile. At this point, it may sit on the editor's desk for weeks—or at least until he can get to it. Once he finally does, and finds that he will be able to turn it into the next bestseller, his excitement turns to sorrow as he reads another letter from you saying that a competing publishing company has bought the book.

You can imagine his frustration. This is why many editors prefer exclusive submissions. Editors want the chance to buy the promising manuscripts waiting on their desks without having to worry that someone else has already signed them. But this isn't quite fair to the writer.

The Writer's Side

Now let's see it from your side. Let's say you have four publishing companies at the top of your list for submissions. You have thoroughly researched each and are confident that your book would fit in well with their lists. However, each requests an exclusive submission.

You finally make your decision on which to send the manuscript to first. That publisher spends four months with your work only to send you a polite letter declining the book. You move on to the next; this one also spends four months and returns the manuscript. On to the third. Again, another four months pass by before you find out the editor doesn't think it would work well on the list. A full year has gone by before you are able to send your manuscript to the fourth publisher. At this rate, you may die of old age before you are able to see your book in print.

ESSENTIAL

Multiple submissions can be a tricky thing. If you are interested in sending out multiple submissions, you may want to divide up your list of potential publishers into small batches of, say, five or six. This will make it easy to keep an eye on who has what and will give you time to revise before sending your manuscript on to the others if the first batch doesn't make a sale.

This is why so many choose to send multiple submissions. Of course, you need to be careful with multiple submissions. You don't want to have your manuscript out with so many publishers that you can't keep them all straight.

Editors sometimes make comments on those manuscripts that are good but not fit for a particular list. If you receive personal comments with a returned manuscript, you should take them very seriously. You will probably want to take these suggestions into consideration and maybe do a little revising before you send the work off to the next publishers on your list.

Tracking Submissions

You will need to keep track of your submissions—especially if you choose to send multiple submissions—for several reasons. First of all, it is just good to know where your manuscript is. By noting the date you sent it, you can keep track of how long it stays with a particular publisher. Second, if your manuscript has been declined several times, you don't want to make the mistake of sending it to a publisher that has already seen it. Finally, if your manuscript is accepted by one publisher and is still out with three others, you will want to let the three publishers know that they need not consider it any longer.

Getting Organized

Set up an organizational system that works for you. Many writers use Excel spreadsheets or Word documents listing all the relevant information. Create a file and e-mail it to yourself—this way it will always be available to you.

Regardless of how you decide to set up your tracking system, there are certain things that you will need to include: title, type of submission (query letter, proposal, full-length manuscript), publisher's name, editor's name (if you have a specific contact name), date sent, date returned, and any comments that accompany the returned manuscript. You may also choose to add information that pertains to each submission. For instance, if you sent along a confirmation postcard, you may want to note the date the editor received the manuscript. Or maybe you decide to send follow-up letters or make phone calls and want to note these as well.

Once you get involved in the submission process, you will be able to design an organizational system that suits your needs. In the meantime, consider using the following table to get you started.

YOUR MANUSCRIPT'S TITLE HERE					
Publisher	Editor	Type of Submission	Date Sent	Date Returned	Additional Comments

CHAPTER 13

Coping with Acceptance or Rejection

So you've followed the submission guidelines, sent your packet off, and waited patiently for what seems like forever. Finally, the fateful day arrives when you go to your mailbox and see the self-addressed stamped envelope you so long ago sent with your manuscript. Inside lies the answer. Will you be published? If not, are you prepared for rejection? Have you made sure that trusted readers have praised your work, and given you confidence, or is your self-esteem riding on this one editor's response?

Exploring the Unknown

Most likely it is not an acceptance letter. Editors or agents usually call or e-mail with good news. But the letter may not be all bad news either. Acceptance and rejection aren't always plain and final. The publisher may see merit in your story and style, but feel that some aspects don't meet their specific publishing goals. You may discover your returned manuscript has been marked up for possible revision.

You could find that an editor has sent you a lengthy letter. The editor first compliments you on your work. Part of an editor's expertise is the ability to see promise despite problems. She may be interested in the book, but asks that you make several revisions before she can offer you a contract.

Good News or Bad News?

An editorial comment letter is good news and bad news. Yes, it means you have much more work ahead of you. But this time, there is encouragement from someone with the power to publish you. That editor wouldn't waste precious time making suggestions if she didn't want to add your book to the list.

FACT

Many writers don't know that an editor doesn't always have the authority to buy a book. Often, an editor must pitch the book to a publication board before she can offer a contract. While editors were once able to buy whatever books they chose, these days everyone wants a piece of the action: production team, art director, sales and marketing, and publicity. Sometimes the marketing department has as much clout as the editor.

You are having mixed emotions about the letter. The editor doesn't guarantee a contract, so why bother reading through the next nine pages and making the suggested revisions? You have already worked so hard on your manuscript, and yet the editor is telling you it still isn't good enough. The editor said "before I can offer you a contract" so that means she is going to offer you a contract, right? Not necessarily. Until you have signed the contract, your book has not been sold.

Too Many Revisions?

If an editor has to get approval before buying a book, she needs to present the very best material possible to her editorial board. Her belief that your manuscript can rise to the appropriate standard is the reason for your entry into the gray area. But be careful how long you remain there. Sometimes you will make the revisions according to the editorial letter, believing your book will be bought, only to receive another letter telling you to make even more revisions. This can be a very stressful experience. At some point you may need to consider whether the changes are improving the book or even moving it closer to contract.

If you are put through three or four rounds of revisions without a contract being offered, you may want to consider whether you should pull the book and try your luck elsewhere. The type of revisions requested should weigh heavily in your decision. They should be specific enough that you can use your creativity to solve the problems; you should not be pulling your hair as you try to decide merely what the editor means. Don't forget, you are always free to ask questions.

Rolling with the Punches

If you receive your manuscript with a plain rejection letter, remember that the work may better fit another publisher's or editor's preferences; don't treat a rejection letter as a completely objective judgment on you as a writer, or on your story, or on your other work, and whatever you do, keep writing. Some of the world's best writers received a series of rejection letters before finally finding a publisher willing to take a chance on them. Also keep in mind that an editor, reading your work for the first time, is in a very different position than a teacher, mentor, or writing peer. Your mentors are concerned with how to encourage you, improve your work, and help you make it publishable. After the publisher has signed you, your editor will have similar goals. But when he sees your work for the first time, his concerns will probably be whether the manuscript fits his company's goals, and whether he feels a special connection to it.

Time spent feeling sorry for yourself and temporarily giving up is time you could better spend improving your manuscript or researching another publisher to send it to. If you have developed good work habits, along with a time and place to go write each day, this will help you move past the momentary emotional setback of a rejection letter. It's not easy, but what is? The rewards of hard work and developing your own creativity are hard to beat—beyond paying the necessary bills, they are actually better than anything money can buy.

ESSENTIAL

Always remind yourself that publishing is business. Even the best-written manuscript may not find a place in the current market. Successful authors often report that not every manuscript they wrote was accepted for publication. It can't be helped, so continue to do your best work: compose, revise carefully, and send it out.

Don't be too proud to take your story to your writing group, a trusted friend, or (for a fee) an editor or teacher and ask, "Should I keep working on this project, or move on to another?" Of course the person you ask could be wrong. But if all opinions point the same way, that can be helpful information.

Taking Rejection Personally

The last thing you want to do is consider a rejection letter a personal insult. There could be twenty reasons why an editor has turned down your work—and none of them may have a thing to do with your writing skills. If you are lucky, you may get a detailed rejection letter explaining why your book does not meet the needs of the company, but quite often you will just receive a form letter that says your manuscript is not suitable for its list.

Stop yourself if you are considering contacting the editor and demanding a good reason for the rejection of your manuscript. This will only serve to give you a reputation as being difficult to work with, not to mention alienating that particular editor. Business is business, and if an editor does not believe he can sell your book, then you'll just have to get over it and move on. But if you receive a tiny bit of encouragement in your letter, a note that says "We enjoyed this but . . ." or the statement "We hope you will send us something in the future," that is actually great news. Take such notes seriously, work hard, and in six months' time send the editor something new, being sure to mention their encouragement in your cover letter.

Using Rejection as Motivation

Some writers find that they simply can't separate emotion from rejection; therefore, they channel that emotion into a motivation tool. Don't laugh—it works. Let's say you receive a couple of rejection letters for a manuscript you know is good. You could use those rejections as excuses to give up, which will get you absolutely nowhere, or you could use the rejections to encourage you to improve upon your story and prove those editors wrong. Determination to make such a statement has helped many writers on difficult days.

FACT

Sometimes an editor will decline a particular manuscript, but like your writing ability and ask you to send in something else. You've got your foot in the door, now get the publisher's catalogue and study it. Try to figure out why your story didn't fit, and why the next one will have a better chance.

Some writers have been known to wallpaper their writing area with rejection letters. That has worked for some people, but it could keep you in a resentful mood during your precious work time. Perhaps a better frame of mind for creative work would flow from a photo or two that bring good memories. You could tack up a clipping of a story that inspires you, or a large sheet of paper with your project's outline.

Degrees of Rejection

A form letter is the most common type of rejection. Publishing companies typically have a standard letter that will say something along the lines of "Thank you for your submission, but your book does not meet our needs." The letter is likely to be addressed to "Dear Author" rather than to you by name. It may not even be signed by a specific editor, instead showing just "Editorial Department" or "Submissions Coordinator" at the bottom.

The only thing you can be sure of is that if you receive one of these letters, your manuscript is not going to be published by that company. The best advice is just to move on.

Personalized Comments

A less painful rejection comes when a standard form letter is marked with additional comments specific to your book. While it doesn't seem like much, a letter like this is worth its weight in gold. This means that an editor was interested enough in your manuscript to take the time, even if it is the smallest amount, to write a letter to you.

ALERT

Even if an editor shows some level of interest in your manuscript, such as sending you a personalized letter, do not make changes and resubmit your manuscript unless you are asked to do so. If an editor takes time out of his busy schedule to give you advice, don't repay the kindness by harassing him with your revised manuscript.

This is special treatment. Think about how easy it would be for an editor to stuff your return envelope with a form letter, or even have someone else do it. Instead, the editor knows she isn't buying your book, but wants to give you a little advice anyway. Read her words carefully. Are the comments something you can use to improve your manuscript before sending it off to another publisher? Pay attention to this type of rejection letter and use it well!

Edited Manuscript

The most encouraging rejection includes a standard letter as well as an edited manuscript. This rarely occurs, but some editors have been known to be so passionate about literature that sometimes they just can't help themselves. If you are one of the lucky few to get such a treat, you absolutely must consider what the editor has done with your manuscript.

Toss aside the feeling of rejection and take notice of the detailed attention your manuscript has received. If you do happen to receive this type of rejection, know what you are holding in your hands.

Too Many Form Letters

There comes a time in nearly every writer's life when he must set aside a project and start afresh. Receiving several impersonal form letters just may be the signal that such a time has come. It is a very difficult decision to make, and one that will probably cause a bit of emotional pain.

Don't think of this as a failure. Instead, think of it as a learning experience. Be proud of yourself for completing a project and taking a chance on its publication. This is a hard step for many writers to take. You have succeeded in facing your fear, and now you are free to start a new project. The more you write, the better you will become.

Revision Required

If you have rejection letters that include specific reasons for the rejection, or advice on how to improve your manuscript, take the time to carefully consider each of these. Are you finding any responses that are similar? Is there a certain comment made about your manuscript across the board? If so, you are in luck. While you may not feel lucky while reading these letters, the comments can help you improve upon the manuscript and give it a better shot at being published.

First, address an issue that is brought up in several different letters. For example, let's say five out of seven rejection letters made a comment referring to the development of your main character. One said that the character is too flat, another said that the character showed no growth or development throughout the story, one said that the character had no flaws, and two simply said that the main character needed work. So what are you going to do with these comments? Well, let's hope you decide to work on your main character before submitting the manuscript anywhere else.

If there is no common issue brought up in the letters, then just take each one at a time and go through the comments. Could any of the comments be used to improve upon your story? If you receive several letters offering advice, it probably means that your story has potential but it's not quite there. Take some time off from the submission process and return to the revision process for a while. Remember that the majority of your reviewers could be wrong; there might be a single letter that rings true, and that speaks to the heart of what your story needs. Pay attention to your writerly intuitions, and to those of the people you consider your most discerning readers.

When Rejections Begin Piling Up

As a first-time writer, you will likely receive several rejection letters, whether form letters or lengthy letters with helpful comments. And while you may come to expect this, you probably can't help wondering if the pile of rejection letters is trying to tell you something. Maybe you aren't cut out for children's writing. Should you really keep trying? Is all the hard work that goes into writing, researching, revising, and submitting just a waste of your time? Before you start second-guessing yourself, think about why you began writing in the first place.

If you truly love writing for children, the pile of rejection letters isn't going to hit quite as hard. On the other hand, if you had dreams of fame and fortune, it is likely you are reconsidering the path you are on. Hopefully, your reasons for writing are true to the craft and will help you get through the hard times.

Oh Happy Day!

We've dealt plenty enough with rejections, let's now move on to the good news—acceptance. That day will come when you hear the phone ring, debate whether or not you should answer it, cringe while picking up the receiver because you are sure it's either a salesperson or a pollster, and then hear that sweet voice saying your story has been accepted. Your family rushes to your side as you hit the floor in a faint. You haven't won the lottery, but you've sold your first book!

The Initial Reaction

Yes, the excitement is churning in your stomach. Yes, you feel like you could scream until there's nothing left of your voice. But the editor is still on the phone waiting for your response. Don't worry; editors have come to expect outbursts of excitement, so it's okay. But do try to remain as calm as possible, at least until you get off the phone.

You should listen carefully to what the editor says next. He will probably explain a little about the process and what you can expect in the following days, weeks, and months. If you have the presence of mind to comprehend what he's saying, great. If not, take notes and worry about them later. You will want to know when you can expect a confirmation letter. If the editor doesn't mention this, you should.

ALERT

Don't let your excitement cause you to forget all your responsibilities. Remember those multiple submissions you sent out? As soon as your contract is signed, you need to withdraw your manuscript from the other publishers. If they choose your book only to find it's not available, they might not talk to you about the next one.

After you have conducted yourself as professionally as possible, immediately call all friends and family members to relay the awesome news. Plan a celebration or just let them come to you. You can either start celebrating that very second or wait a little bit until you have the other formalities out of the way. Some writers can't rest easy until they have signed the contract. Of course, the choice is yours, but know that you will probably have to wait a little while until you receive a copy of the contract, so if you're in a partying mood, by all means get down to it.

It's a Celebration!

It has taken a lot of hard work, heartache, and sacrifice, but you made it. You are about to have your book sitting alongside those of all the other authors in the library. Before you get back to work, take some time to revel in your accomplishment. Jump up and down if you want to. Go in the backyard and scream, or call all your friends over and have a party. When your book comes out, you are going to touch the lives of both children and adults. Your words are going to have an impact on all who read them. You have told your story, and it will be in tangible form for children to hold, parents to read at bedtime, and you to put on display.

While there are no rules regarding the type of celebration, there are rules to be followed during the celebration:

- Do not call the editors who sent you rejection letters and gloat.
- Do not go on a shopping spree buying all your family and friends expensive presents (your advance will not cover this).
- Do not worry about what happens next—contracts, royalty statements, new projects, etc.
- Do not drunk-dial an old flame to let her know what she is missing out on.
- Do have fun.
- Do be proud of your accomplishment.
- Do call yourself an author.
- Do accept compliments gracefully.

That about covers it. Relax and have some fun.

What Comes Next?

After the celebration has died down and the guests have all gone home, you may find yourself lying awake in bed wondering what happens next. Do you need to find a lawyer or agent? What if the deal falls through? After all, you don't have anything in writing, only a telephone call from the editor. How long will it take for your book to reach stores? Does the book need more work? Who will do the illustrations? The questions could go on and on during the wee hours of the morning when nothing is certain.

FACT

It usually takes several months for a book to go from the contract stage to the bookshelves. Don't be discouraged if your editor informs you that your book will not reach the bookstores until the following year. This is fairly standard. Publishing companies have to plan and work well in advance. Once you get to know the processes, you'll understand why.

In the next few chapters we will discuss contracts and the processes your book will go through in the coming months. For now, let's take a look at what you can expect shortly after you receive the news that a publisher has accepted your book.

Confirmation Letter

You will probably first receive a letter confirming that the publisher wants to publish your book and stating that a contract will follow shortly. Or the letter may state that you need to make a few revisions before the publisher can offer a contract. (Your editor most likely gave you this information during the congratulatory phone call.) If you are a first-time writer, it is common practice for an editor to want to see revisions before the contract stage. If you are asked to do revisions, then you will be given a deadline to complete them.

Contract

Once you receive the contract, you may want to hire a lawyer or a literary agent to review it for you. Contracts can be very confusing to someone who doesn't deal with such things on a daily basis. While publishers aren't out there to cheat you, they will ask for more rights than you have to give up. It is always best to know what you're signing. The contract will alert you to issues you need to know about. We'll discuss contracts in greater detail in the next chapter.

Monies

Of course, you can also expect to be paid for your hard work. If you are paid royalties, then you will probably get an advance, which is a set amount of money paid to you before the book earns money. You will be paid royalties only once the advance earns out. In other words, the book must earn enough money to cover your advance payment before you can begin collecting royalty checks. Another form of payment is the flat fee. This is one agreed-upon lump sum that the publisher pays you for the rights to your book. You will not be paid royalties or any other monies, regardless of how well your book sells.

The money you are paid for your book will not have taxes taken out of it. You must pay the taxes yourself. You may want to consult a financial adviser for the best way to do this. But for right now, keep in mind that the full sum you receive is not entirely dispensable; you will need to put some of it aside for taxes.

Take a Deep Breath

While there is certainly a lot to learn about the publishing business, you have time. Don't feel as though you have to know everything up front. Your editor will work with you. Your fellow writers will work with you. Your lawyer or literary agent will work with you. And, of course, you have this book to help you learn.

Don't panic. You've been waiting a long time to get your book published. Just think about all you have learned so far. Apparently you did a great job or you wouldn't have received that congratulatory phone call or e-mail. You will learn as you work your way through the maze. Everything will be a new experience and a lesson learned. Arm yourself with basic knowledge and then learn by doing.

CHAPTER 14

The Writer's Rights

While receiving a contract is very exciting, it can also be overwhelming. There is a lot of legal language and there are complicated publishing terms and phrases. You may decide to hire someone to negotiate for you, but it is important to understand the basics yourself. This chapter will help you learn contract basics and understand some of the writer's rights. If you have an agent or lawyer in the field, she will negotiate to improve your contract. This chapter will help you understand what kinds of changes she can ask for.

An Overview of Contracts

Just as each publisher is different, so are its contracts. Some will be only a page, and others could be forty pages long. While it would be impossible to go into detail about individual contracts here, the following sections should give you a basic understanding of some of the most common elements found in book contracts.

The Author's Duties and Rights

Most contracts will include a description of the work, and you are expected to fulfill this description. This can include the type of work (fiction, nonfiction), format of manuscript, number of pages or word count, and an outline. Of course, there may be other elements included in the description, depending on the publisher. There will also be a deadline date given by which time you must turn in the completed manuscript. Sometimes contracts will also include deadlines for revisions or other such work to the manuscript. The contract can describe how the manuscript is to be delivered on the deadline date, such as in an e-mail attachment, in hard copy, or on disk.

FACT

Usually, a publishing company will have a standard contract, with blank spaces where specifics are filled in, such as title, deadline dates, and compensation. After a negotiation with your agent, attorney, or yourself, some of the paragraphs, such as those claiming your film rights, may be crossed out. Just because a paragraph looks "standard" doesn't mean you must accept it.

The contract will require that you promise not to include any libelous statements about a third party. You are also required to promise that the work is entirely yours and not copied or taken from another source. If you do include material from another source, you must include a citation and provide written permission, which will sometimes involve the payment of a fee to the party that owns the rights to the material. Most publishers will stipulate that you are responsible for this fee. In regard to some children's books, such as how-to books, the contract may require that you have not included anything that may harm the reader.

The copyright should be in your name, unless you have agreed to a work-for-hire project, in which case the publishing company will most likely have the copyright in its name. The publisher will apply for the copyright in your name, but you should insist that your contract specify that this will be done within 90 days of publication. You need the registration in order to collect damages and attorney's fees, in case you have to sue someone for infringement.

Also look for the reversion of rights clause, which stipulates what happens to the rights once a book goes out of print or if the publishing company goes under. These things happen all the time. Pay close attention to the definition of your book staying "in print." In earlier days this meant that the publisher was required to keep physical books available in a warehouse; if no books were printed within a six-month period, rights would revert to the author upon the author's written request. But now, many publishers wish to define "in print" in terms of the book being digitized and stored in a computer. If you sign a contract containing such a definition, your book may become unavailable to the public, but the rights may never revert to you. This means you can't sell them to another publisher, or even print them yourself through a print-on-demand company, to keep them available for fans or students.

Be careful of language like "including but not limited to" and "media now known or hereafter devised." Make sure that each separate right you license to your publisher has specific terms and conditions, after which they revert to you. If your publisher insists on a particular right, offer a compromise: you will license that right for a limited time, say two years.

Your publisher will probably insist on e-book and audiobook rights; you should understand the royalty percentages of these rights. This is a rapidly evolving topic, and you should stay current by discussing it with your agent or attorney and by reading materials from The Authors Guild. Publishers know that in the future digital rights may be very valuable, as books provide content for e-book, audiobook, television, and Internet programming. Some of these applications don't cost the publisher much money to exploit, so you should receive a higher royalty percentage. If a hardcover royalty is 10 percent, and a paperback royalty is 5 percent, perhaps a digital royalty should be in the range of 15 to 25 percent. Sometimes publishers hold on to digital rights forever, and sometimes for five years. The term may be negotiable.

The Publisher's Duties and Rights

The contract will stipulate what the company will pay you for an advance and royalties, as well as what percentage you will take for the sale of subsidiary rights. It will state how many copies of the book you are to receive free of charge, and what price you will pay for additional copies, which is normally at a discounted rate. Or, if this is a work-for-hire, the contract will state the flat fee you are to be paid.

The contract will spell out the handling of rights and what should happen if any rights are sold. Normally, the publisher handles the selling of rights and you are entitled to a percentage of the sale. We will discuss subsidiary rights in further detail in a moment.

Sometimes you will find an option clause in the contract. This clause states that you are required to send your next work to the publisher. The publisher is given the right of first refusal. In other words, you must submit your next work to this publisher and no other until the publisher has declined the manuscript. There are usually no set limits on the time the publisher has to review your next work. So, under contract, your manuscript could be with that publisher for several months before the editor gets to it. If there is not a time limit stipulated, you may find yourself stuck waiting for a response, unable to submit it elsewhere.

This is just an overview of common contract elements. The following sections go into greater detail about those that tend to create the most confusion.

Understanding Royalties

Once you receive a contract, you will probably first flip ahead to the page that states how much you will be paid. After all, you have put a lot of hard work into this manuscript, and though you are pleased that it will be turned into book form, you want to know what your compensation will be. Though your editor has most likely already discussed this with you, it is just a good feeling to see it in writing.

There are two basic types of compensation: flat fee and royalty basis. The flat fee is given in cases of a work-for-hire. This is pretty straightforward: you are paid a set amount of money for writing a book and turning over all rights to the book. You do not receive any further payments.

On the other hand, if you signed a contract to receive royalties, then you will receive royalty statements detailing what monies you are entitled to. They will show how your book is selling and the amount of royalties being paid to you, based on the percentage agreed upon in the contract. Check these statements carefully to be sure you are getting what you deserve. While a publishing company is not likely to cheat you, mistakes can be made. Your agent will be better prepared to interpret royalty statements than you are. Also keep in mind that while you may have earned the money several months earlier, the check may take a while to get to you. Normally, publishing companies cut royalty checks twice a year, some annually.

The Advance

The advance is just what it sounds like—an advance payment on the money you will earn from the sales of your book.

Let's say you have written a middle-grade novel. The contract states that you will be given an advance of $4,000 for this manuscript, half to be paid on signing of the contract and the other half to be paid when the manuscript has been received and deemed acceptable (acceptable meaning that you have fulfilled your contractual obligations, in the judgment of your editor).

ALERT

If you have written a picture book that was illustrated by someone else, then you will have to split the royalties with the illustrator. Normally the royalties are divided equally. So if the book had been receiving a 10 percent royalty, then you would be paid a 5 percent royalty.

This is money you would be entitled to once your book is published and begins selling. Your book must earn back the advance before you can begin collecting royalties on it. In the above case, your novel must earn $4,000 in royalties before you get any more money.

Royalty Calculations

Royalties are traditionally paid on the list price (suggested retail price) of the book, which means the price you would pay as a customer buying the book. Some companies do, however, pay royalties based on the net price, or the amount of money the publisher retains on each book after expenses. Net price takes into consideration discounts that are often offered to buyers, which can come down below half the retail price, as well as other expenses to the publisher. If the publisher has the right to calculate net, and pays you on that basis, then the possibility of your evaluating the fairness of your statements is reduced. To compensate for these factors, your royalty percentage should be higher if it is based on net than if it is based on list.

Let's say your middle-grade novel will earn royalties based on the list price. To keep things simple, we'll say that your novel's retail price is $10. Your contract states that you will receive a 10 percent royalty on hardcover editions. So, for this example, you would receive $1 per hardcover book sold. Now, you need to figure in the advance:

Advance (4,000) divided by royalty per book (1) equals number of books to be sold before the advance earns out (4,000).

Before you will receive any more money, your book must sell 4,000 copies. Beginning with copy number 4,001, you will begin receiving $1 per book sold.

To make this even more complicated, paperback editions of hardcover books normally have a smaller royalty even though the text is exactly the same. Publishers have to do this because the retail price for paperbacks is lower but the costs to produce the book are still high.

ESSENTIAL

You may want to inquire about an escalator clause in your contract. An escalator clause states that once your book sells beyond a set number, the royalties will increase. It certainly doesn't hurt to ask. Check with your agent about the possibility of negotiating for this.

Let's say the contract states that you will receive a 6 percent royalty on the paperback edition of your book. So if the paperback edition of your book sold for $5, then you will receive 30 cents per book sold. In this example, you would not need to calculate in the advance since the hardcover edition had already earned out the advance. But what if it hasn't? Sometimes the contract will specify that the paperback sales must pay back the advance, if the hardcover hasn't done so. This could be a negotiating point.

You can already see some of the complexities of contracts. If you landed your book deal without an agent, you might want to get one at this stage, to help you understand and negotiate the contract being offered. Also, at the moment you are offered a contract, you are eligible to join The Authors Guild (*www.authorsguild.org*); they will provide much information about contracts. They are very tough advocates for writers, and you may not want to be as demanding as they suggest, but they are on your side, and they will help you understand the issues.

Subsidiary Rights

"Subsidiary rights" is a general term used to refer to all rights to a manuscript other than the initial publication rights. You're probably wondering, what else is there? Well, there's a lot. It's important that you understand what is outlined in the contract regarding subsidiary rights—who has the authority to sell these rights and what percentage of the sales you will get.

How many times have you seen a movie that was based on a book? This falls under the subsidiary rights clause in your contract. Remember, this is your creation. If others want to profit off of it, then you are entitled to a cut. In addition to movie rights, subsidiary rights include:

- **Foreign language translations** (as well as publication in foreign countries that also speak English). Only give these rights to the publisher if it can demonstrate the ability to exploit them. Otherwise, your agent may do a better job for you, and you will not need to share the revenue with your publisher. Often agencies partner with other agencies in various countries in order to bring foreign marketing expertise to your book.
- **Television, radio, and theater**—any type of performance art. Do not automatically give these rights to your publisher. Maybe you have connections in television; maybe your agent has connections in theater. Try to negotiate a contract which allows you, your agent, and the publisher to seek performance opportunities.

- **First serial** (publication in periodicals before the book is published). Normally the publisher will be allowed to negotiate publication of part of your book in a magazine, for example, but monies collected should be divided heavily in your favor.
- **Second serial** (publication in periodicals after the book is published). If you give your publisher this right, limit it to a certain time period.
- **Book clubs.** Normally your publisher will take these rights and will be able to exploit them for you.
- **Anthologies.** Once your story is published, you should retain the right to license it for inclusion in an anthology. Some stories will have a long life, and appear in several anthologies. You (and your agent) will get paid each time, but your original publisher should not.
- **Textbooks.** You should try to retain rights to license your work for inclusion within a textbook.
- **Large print editions.** Normally your publisher will retain these rights and exploit them for you, but discuss this with your agent.
- **Audio versions.** The publisher will want these rights, but limit the term to a set period, such as two years.
- **Electronic.** The publisher will demand these. Try to limit the term, and be vigilant about royalty amounts.
- **Merchandising** (any consumer product that is based on your story or characters, such as a stuffed animal or game). Discuss with your agent the possibility of retaining these rights.

FACT

While subsidiary rights often refer to media other than books, they refer to paperback books as well—both mass-market and trade. Publishing companies frequently publish the paperback versions of their hardcover titles, but they don't have to. They can sell these rights to another publishing company.

If you are unsure of what these rights may or may not include, be sure to ask. If you have an agent, the agent will most likely negotiate the contract to keep some of the rights with the agency. The agent will then work to sell these rights—of course, taking a 15 percent commission. If you use an entertainment lawyer, she will charge a flat fee or hourly fee for the work, but will not retain that 15 percent in the property in the future.

One new and very important area of subsidiary rights is digital rights. This includes the right to market your book in an electronic reader, as an e-book. This market is new but growing fast, and you can expect it to become a major factor in book contracts over the next few years. Study materials from The Authors Guild before you sign away your digital rights.

Copyright 101

Some first-time writers are concerned that someone will steal their story and publish it as their own. For this reason, they apply for a copyright through the U.S. Copyright Office before sending in the manuscript. While it may sound like a great idea, it is unnecessary. In fact, editors who see the copyright symbol (©) on a submitted manuscript will likely deem the writer an amateur.

By simply writing your work, you are copyrighting it. That's the beauty of the copyright law. Once you have put your idea into tangible or "fixed" form, in this case on paper in written form, the work is automatically protected under law. Copyright protects both published and unpublished works. You needn't go through the hassle of contacting the office, requesting the needed materials, and filling out the appropriate forms. Once your manuscript has been accepted for publication, the publishing company will do that for you. But as mentioned above, add a clause to your contract that the publisher will register your copyright within 90 days, just in case you become involved in a lawsuit.

Ideas Are Not Protected

On the other hand, someone could steal your idea. Ideas are not protected under copyright law. If they were, there would be very few books ever published. For instance, let's say you have an idea for a story in which the protagonist braves a fierce thunderstorm and miraculously pulls through. As your idea, it may seem like something no one has ever published before—taking into consideration specific details, characterizations, and settings.

However, take the idea to its very foundation—man versus nature—and then think of all the books published with that same idea in mind. See, it's really not that original. It is how you present the idea and tell the story that makes your work unique and therefore able to be protected.

FACT

The publishing company is not required under law to display a copyright notice. Don't worry; it is still protected. However, you don't want someone to steal your work and then claim they didn't know it was under copyright. So even though it isn't necessary, it is still important to inform the public of the copyright status.

How Long Does the Protection Last?

Not to interrupt your huge sigh of relief, but copyright does not protect your work forever. The U.S. Copyright Office states on its website (*www.loc.gov/copyright*) that a work "created on or after January 1, 1978, is automatically protected from the moment of its creation and is ordinarily given a term enduring for the author's life plus an additional seventy years after the author's death." So what happens to your work once it is no longer protected by copyright? It enters the public domain.

Public Domain

Once a work is no longer protected by copyright, it passes into the public domain. This means that anyone can use the work in whatever way he wants without having to pay for permission to use it. The author and the author's heirs do not receive any type of payment for its use.

For instance, think about all the reproductions of Edgar Allan Poe's work. His works have taken form in textbooks, books of individual stories, compilations of his selected works, anthologies, and movies. Because his work is in the public domain, publishers, movie producers, editors of anthologies, and so forth can use his material to make a nice profit. They are paying only production costs because they do not have to pay the author for the right to use the work.

A Twist on the Original

You aren't a publisher or movie producer, so how can you use the works in the public domain to your advantage? Well, you could use a work that is in the public domain and add a new twist to it, narrate it from a different character's point of view, provide a sequel to the story, or adapt it into a modern version.

Perhaps you have read a story and, while thoroughly enjoying it, questioned several of its ingredients. Maybe these questions have haunted you, so you make an attempt to answer them in your own style. The beginnings of your own fantastic tale are indebted to the original work. You may choose to go into depth about the main character's childhood, perhaps explaining some of his actions in the original story. Or maybe you continue the story into the character's adulthood.

Maybe, as a child, you read a classic tale differently than other kids. Maybe you sympathized with the antagonist, and didn't care for the main character. You could recreate the story shedding light on the antagonist's feelings, and turn the story around to make the original antagonist the protagonist.

The possibilities are endless. But if you are considering using a work that is in the public domain to your advantage, you need to see who else out there has had the same idea. For example, if you were fascinated with the wolf from *The Three Little Pigs* and want to tell his version of the story, you will soon find that this has already been done in *The True Story of the 3 Little Pigs,* by Jon Scieszka.

Plagiarism, Permissions, and Fair Use

Now that you know what is and isn't protected by copyright, we'll talk a little about the in-between stuff. In some cases, you will be able to use someone else's work even though it is copyrighted. It's important to pay for most uses, and the responsibility for getting permissions usually falls on the author. When you use a few lines from a poem or song, you must consider what percentage of the whole you are borrowing. The trend seems to be that publishers are becoming more cautious about quotations, and licensing them is becoming more expensive.

Plagiarism

The illegal way to use someone else's work is to plagiarize. Plagiarism is taking someone else's words or ideas and passing them off as your own. Under no circumstances should you ever plagiarize. Even if you use material that falls under fair use, you must always cite the source. Otherwise, it is plagiarism, and in this technological age, plagiarists are sure to get caught.

Plagiarism is considered literary theft and taken very seriously. Always check with your editor if you are concerned about your use of someone else's work. To be completely on the safe side, create an original work and don't rely on the words of others.

Permissions

If the material you want to include does not fall under fair use, then you will need to be granted permission for the use of the material. For instance, let's say you are writing a nonfiction piece on losing a parent. You have discovered a wonderful article published in a well-known and respected psychology journal that you wish to quote. The excerpt you want to use is straightforward and clearly written—and two paragraphs long. In this case, you would want to get permission to use the excerpt in your book.

You would have to pay for the use of the excerpt and get the permission in writing. Often publishing companies will require a copy of the permission to keep in your file if you are using excerpted material. In fact, the contract will sometimes have a clause involving permissions and who is responsible for acquiring and paying for them (this usually falls to the author).

Also be sure to give credit where credit is due. If you are copying the material word for word, use quotation marks, and don't forget to cite your source.

Fair Use

If the use of another author's words falls under fair use, then you are fine. You won't have to pay for the right to use them; neither will you have to go to jail. So what is fair use? Unfortunately, this category is not easily defined.

Generally speaking, you may use a very small percentage of a whole copyrighted work. So if you want to quote a phrase or sentence from a 500-page book, this would be considered fair use—if, and only if, you cite the source. If you do not cite the source and use a direct quote, passing it off as your own words, then it is considered plagiarism.

Remember, it must be a small piece of the whole. Let's say you want to use a single line from a poem. While this may not seem like much, if the poem is only three lines long, you have taken 33 percent of the author's work, which certainly does not categorize it as fair use.

This chapter has explained some of the rights of authors and publishers, and some areas in which these rights can be negotiated. Rights issues are complex and changing, and you need to educate yourself well before you receive that first contract. As soon as you are eligible, join The Authors Guild and study their materials. You're about to be a published author; arm yourself!

CHAPTER 15

The Editorial Process

After your manuscript has been submitted and accepted, it may be quite a while before you see it again. Publishing companies are, in some ways, designed as factories. To make sure books do not hit the shelves with mistakes in them, specific editorial duties are assigned to different experts, and each one in turn reads a manuscript with their one specialty in mind. For examples, fact-checkers make sure nonfiction books are accurate, copyeditors look for textual inconsistencies and confusions, and structural editors make sure the book flows smoothly. All of these people play essential roles in the editorial process. This chapter will guide you through each of those roles, and through your ongoing duties, as writer, during the process.

Your Main Contact

Up until now, you have probably been dealing with only one person directly—an acquisitions editor. An acquisitions editor's job, on a very basic level, is to acquire books.

Acquisitions editors have to sift through piles of submitted manuscripts every day. Sometimes they will have an assistant do this for them, since the piles can take up quite a bit of time. The assistant or editor will weed out the unacceptable manuscripts and set aside promising ones. From this narrowed group, the editor will choose the manuscripts she believes will make good additions to the company's list.

Pitching to the Pub Board

These days, acquisitions editors are rarely responsible for the final decision. Several staff members must all agree before a book is purchased, which means that the acquisitions editor will have to pitch the manuscript to a team of staff members at a publication board meeting. Because this is the selling point for the manuscript, the editor must be prepared to give it a very strong sales pitch.

FACT

The acquisitions editor will act as the liaison between you and the publishing company. It is not likely that you will have contact with all those people who work on the production of your work. If you have questions about the different phases your manuscript goes through, you should contact your acquisitions editor first instead of trying to track down the art director or publicist.

The editor may request several revisions from the author before taking the manuscript to the publication board. If the manuscript is in good shape, the editor may choose to postpone the revision process until after the board has accepted the manuscript. Even in these cases, there is a ton of work to be done by the acquisitions editor to sell the book. She must gather information about competitive titles and how well they are selling, and collect pertinent market information and reasons why this book would be a good addition to the list, any biographical information about the author that may work as a strong selling point, and any other information that will help convince the publication board to vote yes.

In addition to all of this research information, the editor must also present an idea of what the final product will look like. For instance, she will need to decide whether the book should be hardcover or paperback, what the trim size should be, how many pages and the type of binding the book will have, what the title will be, and any other details that pertain to the book.

As you can see, the acquisitions editor works hard to sell and support those manuscripts she believes the publisher should add to its list. But the acquisitions editor's work doesn't stop there.

Back to the Author

The acquisitions editor then has the pleasure of informing the author that the company wishes to publish the manuscript. After suffering minor loss of hearing when the author screams in her ear, the editor will explain what is to happen with the manuscript. The editor will work with the legal department to produce an appropriate contract, which she will send to the writer. Once the contract has been signed and returned by the author, the editor will usually take it to her superior for approval and signature. With the contract out of the way, the editor will work with the author to revise and restructure the manuscript to get it into the very best shape possible.

The acquisitions editor usually has the responsibility of writing catalog and back cover copy, and sometimes flap copy. Catalog copy is the text that accompanies your book in the publishing company's catalog, which is used by the sales department to pitch the list to buyers. Back cover copy is the text on the back of the book. If the book is hardcover and will have a jacket, the editor must also sometimes write flap copy, which is the text on the inside flap of the jacket. Sometimes the text for all three types of copy is the same; sometimes it isn't. In any case, your editor must craft compelling copy to help sell your book.

This is a summary of what an acquisitions editor does. There are usually more duties beyond those just described, and publishing houses require their acquisitions editors to perform various tasks beyond even those associated with the role of editor. For example, an acquisitions editor may manage a book series, and so her role will include some contract negotiations, author correspondence, etc., in addition to editing.

Types of Editing

Even though your manuscript has been accepted, you will need to make revisions after you sign the contract. In most cases, your acquisitions editor will request the first changes after he does a thorough read-through of the text. Additional editors may request more revisions later, although these may come to you through the acquisitions editor (your main contact) as well.

On the one hand, you certainly want to listen to the advice and suggestions your editor makes for revisions. After all, this is the editor's job. The editor is paid for his knowledge and experience, so don't be afraid to use his expertise to benefit your manuscript. The fact is that sales figures from your first book will affect what future contracts you are offered, and doing what your editor says will maximize your chances of publishing a successful first book.

ESSENTIAL

While you may be involved in the editorial process—making revisions, checking proofs, etc.—this is not always the case, depending on the procedures of the publishing company. If you have agreed to a work-for-hire contract, the publisher will sometimes stipulate that it has say over all changes that need to be made, giving you no authority over what happens to the manuscript after you turn it in.

On the other hand, you need to keep in mind that this is your story. Do not scramble to make every little suggested revision before you have really thought about what you are changing. If you agree with the suggestions and feel that they will improve your manuscript, then by all means, implement them. Whether or not you eventually accept each revision, try to understand why your editor has recommended them. You may find that your editor has considered an angle you have missed, or that his changes will help clarify your ideas to the reader.

Depending on what type of book you have written and how the publishing company is staffed, your manuscript may pass through not only the acquisitions editor's hands but also the developmental editor's hands for revisions. In children's book publishing, the acquisitions editor frequently makes the initial edits himself. There are two different types of editing completed in this first phase.

Structural or Developmental Editing

If you recall, in Chapter 8 you put your manuscript through three different stages of revision. During the first read-through, you looked at the manuscript as a whole and focused on structure and content. This is called structural, or developmental, editing and is the first phase of editing the publisher will put your manuscript through.

Basically, the developmental editor will check the organization and consistency of the manuscript. Let's say your manuscript begins with two chapters giving background information about the characters and establishing the setting in great detail. The developmental editor may decide that the story would work better if you cut these and began instead with the third chapter, which is where the action begins. The editor may ask you to integrate some of the information from the two chapters throughout the first half of the manuscript, and delete any other information from the first two chapters that is not essential to the story line.

This is just one example of what a developmental editor does. She will also look for consistency in character descriptions, flesh out any confusing parts of the manuscript, watch for unintentional tense or point-of-view changes, check the breakdown of chapters, and view the manuscript in terms of the "big picture." The editor will usually write an editorial letter to the author addressing any issues, asking questions, and making suggestions. The revision is then left up to the author.

Line Editing

Once the author turns in a revised manuscript meeting the developmental editor's needs, the manuscript goes through a line edit. While structural editing views the manuscript as a whole, line editing views it line by line. This is where the nitty-gritty work begins.

The editor will be looking at individual lines or sentences to see how well they are structured on their own and in conjunction with the surrounding sentences. The editor will probably first consider whether the sentence has any unnecessary words, whether it is too long or too short, and if it is clear and concise. Are the best words chosen? Is the writing in active voice, or does it fall into passive voice? The editor will then read the sentences surrounding it. Do they all flow smoothly together? Is there a rhythm to their flow, or are they choppy? Does the sentence relate to the others in a sensible and logical way, or does it stand out on its own?

The editor will probably make suggestions for revision directly on the hard copy of the manuscript or by using the track changes feature on the computer. He may include an editorial letter with the manuscript if there are substantial changes that need to be made or if there is something needing detailed explanation. But for the most part, the author will be working off of the actual manuscript, rather than from an editorial letter, because the changes made during line editing are normally smaller and more succinct than those made during structural editing.

The Next Line of Defense: Copyeditors

The copyeditor checks grammar, punctuation, and spelling, and makes sure the text corresponds with the house style.

QUESTION

What is house style?
A publishing company will normally follow the *Chicago Manual of Style*'s rules for grammar and flow. However, publishing companies may differ on a small list of style issues. For instance, one publishing company may use *E-mail*, another may use *email,* and yet another may use *e-mail*. Variances are established in the company's house style.

While your acquisitions editor may have done both structural and line editing, he will not do copyediting. Copyediting requires a different mindset from the other two types of editing. A copyeditor must be detail-oriented and able to focus on one word at a time. Since it is extremely difficult to copyedit your own work, professional copyeditors are truly invaluable.

A publishing company usually has a copy chief who traffics the manuscripts through to the copyeditors. While a company may have copyeditors on staff, many hire freelance copyeditors as well. Because every manuscript the company publishes must go through copyediting, this process can sometimes take several weeks to complete.

It is highly unlikely that you will have any contact with the copyeditor; you probably won't even know his name. Remember, your primary connection with the publishing company lies with the acquisitions editor. When the manuscript has been copyedited and is ready for your review, the acquisitions editor will typically be the one to send it to you.

ESSENTIAL

Having a copyeditor go over your work with a fine-tooth comb is a blessing, so don't complain that the editor's work is too nitpicky. The copyeditor is doing you a tremendous service by making your manuscript read as if you have perfect command of the English language.

As in line editing, the copyeditor will mark changes directly on the manuscript, or using track changes. You will be asked to review the changes made by the copyeditor. Often the changes are simply corrections of grammar, punctuation, and spelling. However, sometimes a copyeditor will revise phrases or query the author about inconsistencies or unclear sections. If you disagree with a change or do not understand a query, talk to your acquisitions editor about it.

The copyeditor is most likely going to be the last person who edits your text. This is also the last time that you will be able to make changes to the text without it costing you. Carefully peruse a copyedited manuscript and make sure that it meets your final approval.

Fact-Checking or Technical Review

If you have written a nonfiction book, your work may also be run by a fact-checker or technical reviewer, whose job it is to verify the accuracy of the text.

This isn't meant to insult you. Obviously the publisher trusts in your abilities, or else you wouldn't have been hired to write the book. But everyone makes mistakes, and an extra pair of eyes never hurt a manuscript.

Fact-checkers and technical reviewers have different, but related, duties. Many books will be edited by one or the other, but usually not by both.

Fact-Checking

Fact-checking is the process of verifying the accuracy of each and every fact within a manuscript. Copyeditors usually make great fact-checkers, because both jobs require extreme attention to detail. Copyeditors are already tuned into minute details and can pick up on the smallest inconsistency. For this reason, some publishing companies will ask a copyeditor to fact-check the manuscript. Sometimes they are asked to do this while copyediting, though this double duty can result in mistakes. If a copyeditor must check grammar, style, punctuation, and spelling, and also facts, both areas could suffer. To ensure that the manuscript receives maximum attention, publishing companies often send manuscripts to a second copyeditor for the sole purpose of fact-checking.

FACT

Some types of fiction are also put through fact-checking. For instance, if you have written a period piece or historical fiction, then the book will include factual accounts and descriptions to set up the story. Books that rely on facts will most likely be sent to a fact-checker.

The fact-checker will rely heavily on your sources and have a few sources of her own. She will mark inconsistencies or false accounts and correct them. You will be sent the completed manuscript and asked to make the necessary changes, just as you would for a copyedited manuscript.

For shorter children's books, fact-checking will not take much time, even though it is a process of singling out every fact and checking it before moving on to the next. For longer books, this can become very time-consuming, and therefore expensive. In these cases, the publisher may choose to send the manuscript to a technical reviewer instead.

Technical Review

The technical review is a form of fact-checking, although it does not involve the tedious process of checking each and every individual fact. Instead, a manuscript in need of a technical review will be sent to a specialist on the particular subject matter of the book.

Let's say you have written a book about making hats. It is likely that the publisher would try to hire a professional milliner or experienced hat shop owner to review the manuscript. Perhaps you have written a how-to book on playing the piano. A publisher may seek out a professional pianist or piano instructor to give the book a technical review.

The technical reviewer won't check every fact for accuracy. Rather, he will read the manuscript as a whole and rely on his expertise to flag any inaccuracies. Again, the technical reviewer will probably highlight the inaccuracy and correct the problem directly on the manuscript. The author then makes the necessary changes.

Proofreading

While proofreaders don't enter the scene until the book has already been typeset, we'll include them here since they are dealing directly with the text and are part of the editorial group. The proofreader's job is to check the set of proofs (the typeset book) to make sure that all corrections have found their way into this stage.

ESSENTIAL

You have probably heard of proofreaders' marks. These marks are what editors use to make corrections to text. If you receive a copyedited manuscript with proofreaders' marks, don't panic. You can find a list of these marks and what they mean in *The Chicago Manual of Style* and in most large dictionaries.

The proofreader checks the proofs against the copyedited manuscript for any errors made by the typesetter, such as a repeated paragraph or omitted word. She then sends the corrected set back to the copy chief.

During the proofreading stage, you will receive your own set of proofs. This is the very last stage during which you can make corrections. You will be given a deadline to get in your corrected proofs. Do not miss this deadline. If the acquisitions editor does not receive your returned set, she will assume that the proofs are to your liking and you won't be able to make changes later.

Authors are usually allowed a small number of corrections that will be made at no charge, but going above that number will cost you, since it costs the publisher to make changes. When you return the proofs to your acquisitions editor, your changes will be added to the master set, along with the proofreader's corrections, and sent back for correction. Your changes will be marked with "AA," which stands for author alteration. If you have made more changes than allowed, you will be charged for these additional corrections and the amount will likely be deducted from your first royalty statement.

The Waiting Room

While you may have some involvement in the editorial process, the different phases your book goes through may each take several weeks. So what are you supposed to do in the meantime? If this is your first book, you may be anxiously waiting to see this one all the way through before starting a new project. The waiting period after you've submitted your revisions can be tough.

Start a New Project

Your best bet is to go ahead and start something new. Hopefully, you already have several ideas in mind—maybe you have already started getting them down on paper. This is the perfect time to revisit your ideas file and begin the writing process anew.

By spending your time gathering information, writing, rewriting, and enjoying writing, time will slip by. Those weeks of no news about your manuscript will seem like minutes (well, hours, anyway). It is likely that just as you get in the groove of writing for your next project, the acquisitions editor will call on you to check the copyedited manuscript or go over proofs.

Talk to Your Editor

Now that you have established a relationship with someone in a position to help you out, you can talk to your editor directly about future projects. Feel out your editor to see if she is interested in seeing more of your work. Editors like to build relationships with good writers whom they can count on for quality work.

If you have a close relationship, your editor may have already requested work from you. If you have a very close relationship, then you probably already know what her interests are from just everyday chitchat. She may have acquired your first book because she admired the passion you brought to a subject, even if it wasn't one of normal interest to her. Now that you know where her real interests lie, channel your passion and creativity into a new proposal she is likely to find interesting.

Get to work. You now know what to expect from an editor and what an editor expects from you. Use this knowledge to your advantage. Keep in mind that writing is an ongoing learning experience. The more you absorb, the better you will be, and the more books you will sell.

CHAPTER 16

The Production Process

The editorial team members (and you!) have worked magic, and the text is all ready to go. Now you need to kick back, relax, and wait for the bound book to arrive on your doorstep. But how does the edited text actually become a book? This chapter will take you through the production process. You may be surprised at how many talented and technically trained people have key roles in creating the book from your manuscript.

Elements of a Book

Before we actually meet the production team and watch them slowly turn text into a bound book, you need to fully understand all the elements of a book so you can better appreciate how much thought and hard work goes into each completed product. Let's start with the inside and work our way out.

Front Matter

Grab the nearest children's book and open it up. What you will usually see first is the other side of the front cover with paper pasted down on it and a facing blank page. Publishers will decorate these with illustrations or colored paper or just keep them blank.

Now turn the page. This next spread (two facing pages) will usually have a blank verso (left-hand page). The recto (right-hand page) is the title page. The title page includes—you guessed it—the title of the book, the author's name, the illustrator's name, and the publisher's name.

When you turn this page, you'll see the copyright page (verso). This page includes important information, such as who holds the copyright to the book and the illustrations, the copyright dates, the name and address of the publisher, where the book was printed, the publishing history of the book, the ISBN, and the Library of Congress Cataloging-in-Publication Data. The copyright page may also include other information, such as acknowledgments of permissions or a disclaimer.

QUESTION

What is the Library of Congress Cataloging-in-Publication Data?
This is usually referred to as CIP. The publisher must send in a form with the book's information to the Library of Congress. The Library of Congress then classifies the book and creates a record of the information. Libraries nationwide will use this information in their cataloging systems.

The publisher may also have separate pages for a dedication, acknowledgments, preface, or foreword, or the publisher may choose to combine some of these elements onto one page. If the book has chapters, a table of contents will be included in the front matter.

The Body

Following the front matter is the text, usually on a recto. If the book has chapters, a chapter title or number (or both) will begin the text. Each chapter normally starts on a new page. Some publishers open each new chapter on a right-hand page, and others start a new chapter on whichever page comes next. Some publishers decide to begin the chapter at the top of the page, while others begin halfway down the page.

If the book doesn't have chapters, the publisher will sometimes add a drop cap to the first letter of the text. The drop cap makes that first letter larger than the rest of the text and sometimes takes up two lines or more in height. Or the publisher may just choose to start the text right away without any fancy elements.

The body of the book will likely have page numbers. It may also include running heads or feet. A running head (or foot) is the information that is printed across the top (or bottom) of each page of the body. The running head or foot may include the author's name, the title of the book, the title or number of the chapter, or a combination of these. Chapter opening pages can sometimes lack page numbers, running heads, or feet.

Several decisions have to be made about the text itself, but we'll get to that in a moment.

FACT

A publishing company may choose to lay out the insides of a book in any number of ways. For instance, the copyright page may be the verso, while the title page is the recto of the spread. Board books may not have any front matter, and picture books may not have any back matter. Several factors go into the company's decisions regarding the design and layout of each book, all in an effort to make the book the best it can be.

Back Matter

The back matter follows the body of the text. The back matter could include a number of things, depending on the type of book you have written. Some common elements of back matter include: appendix, index, glossary, colophon (information about the production of the book, such as the name of the designer or what medium the illustrator used), and bibliography.

Following the back matter information, the very last spread will often copy that of the very first spread with the same design or color of paper used. And that's it! As you can see, a lot goes into the innards of a book. Now let's take a look at the outside.

The Look

The outside of a book requires a lot of planning. While it may not seem like much—just a front cover, back cover, and spine—this could very well be one of the most complicated elements of the book. The cover is what people are going to see first. If they don't like the looks of the cover, chances are they won't bother finding out what's inside. The cover is one of the primary selling tools of the book. It must be perfect.

The company will probably decide to publish your book in hardcover first. Sometimes a hardcover book won't have anything at all printed on the front and back covers. The spine will have the title of the book, the author's name, and the publisher's name. This is common in adult books. Children's books, however, will sometimes print the same design from the jacket directly on the hardcover.

A jacket will cover the hardcover, adding extra protection. For the prices we pay for hardcovers, we certainly should get a little more. The front of the jacket will have a design that identifies the book, the title, the author's name, the illustrator's name, and mention of any awards the book may have won. The front flap of the jacket will contain promotional copy, usually giving a brief description of the plot, and sometimes the back flap will contain the author's and illustrator's bios. The back of the jacket will include the ISBN, bar code, and price, and sometimes the publisher's name. You will occasionally find some promotional copy on the back of the jacket, such as quotes of praise the book has received. These might be excerpts from reviews, or blurbs contributed by writers in the field.

Paperback covers include the same information you find on a hardcover's jacket, but it's printed directly on the cover. If a publishing company prints a paperback edition following a hardcover edition, the covers of these two books may or may not be the same.

The Art of Design

Now that you know what all the elements in a book are, let's discuss how the book comes together to incorporate those elements. The art director has already developed a schedule for the books coming up, far in advance. He has assigned a designer to each book and will oversee their work. Sometimes a publishing company will have its own team of designers and equipment for the layout; others will freelance this work out on a contract basis.

ESSENTIAL

The best way to get a grasp on design is to look at several different children's books. Look at the differences and similarities between books published by the same company. Also compare the books of one company with those of other companies. Are books designed differently according to category (picture book, early reader, chapter book, middle-grade, and young adult)?

The Designer's Job

First of all, the designer must know the trim size and page count for the book. This will tell the designer how much room she has to work with. The designer will then experiment with margin and gutter widths, fonts and their sizes, and leading (pronounced LED-ING; this is the amount of space between lines) to make the text fit in the allotted number of pages. All these components will either increase or decrease the amount of space the text takes up. The designer must also take into consideration the target age group. Early readers, as you know, will have a lot of white space on the page. Young adult books will have smaller type and little white space.

The designer must decide on the display fonts as well, such as for chapter titles. Speaking of chapter titles, the designer must decide how far down the page the chapter title will be placed and then how far from the chapter title the text will begin. The designer must decide where to place page numbers and where to place running heads or feet (right, left, or center).

A designer also has the responsibility of creating a cover design. As already mentioned, the cover design is very important because it influences the buyer's first impression of the book. The designer may create several different cover designs for the same book. Because it is such an important aspect, a meeting will usually be called to get different opinions before a final decision is made.

ALERT

Do not try to contact the designer about your book. As mentioned earlier, it is unlikely that you will have much involvement in the production process, so if you try to force your ideas on a member of the production team, it will undoubtedly get back to your acquisitions editor. You will be regarded as difficult to work with, hindering your chances for future publication with the company.

Adding Illustrations

If your book has illustrations, you as the author will have very little say in the choice of an illustrator. The illustrator will go through a process of submitting roughs to the art director to get approval before completing the pieces. Once the art is completed, it will be scanned and then incorporated into the layout. Of course, the designer assigned to your book will play a role in this process.

If the designer is working with a picture book, she must decide where the illustration will be placed on the page in conjunction with the text. Look at the various picture books at your disposal. Compare the layouts. Some will have text that runs along the bottom of the page with the illustration taking up the biggest portion of the page. Some will have the text running along the top. Some will place the text within the illustration. And some will use a combination of these. Also look at the sizes of the illustrations. There is a lot of variety in the layout of text with illustrations. The final decision about these things is most often in the hands of the designer with input from the art director.

The Production Manager

The production manager has the important job of making sure your manuscript makes it to tangible book form. He begins plans for your book long before he actually receives it. Because the production manager oversees all books on any given list, he will have scheduled the printing of your book, as well as others, in advance of having it land on his desk. Once the production manager does receive it, he will send it off to the printer on the appointed date, ensuring a smooth and timely printing schedule.

While this may not seem like such a big job, the production manager has a lot more to do than just coordinate printing schedules. One thing to keep in mind, while reading about the role of a production manager, is that this person has the added struggle of staying within a set budget for each book. This will heavily influence most of the production manager's decisions and sometimes cause him to find creative ways of getting what's needed for the money that's been budgeted.

The Printer

One of the major decisions the production manager must make is which printer to select. Usually, the production manager will have a good relationship with several different printers, having worked with them in the past and on a regular basis. If this is the case, the decision may not be too difficult. However, if the budget for a particular book is lower than usual, or if a new printer has caught his eye, the production manager will need to do a lot of research about pricing and quality, getting information from various printers.

FACT

Sometimes a publishing company will choose to have a book printed in a different country. This is usually due to lower printing costs. However, this will increase the time needed for the printing schedule, as it can take longer to ship the book abroad than it would to send it to a domestic printer.

The production manager should be familiar with the capabilities of the printer's equipment and the quality of work it produces. The production manager should also know what the printer's needs are regarding submitted materials and advance scheduling. And, of course, the production manager must know the printing costs.

Paper Choices

Another major decision a production manager must make is what type of paper to use. While you may think paper is paper, it isn't as simple as that. There are several different kinds of paper a book may be printed on. Take a look at a variety of children's books. Can you feel the differences in quality and texture of the papers used?

For instance, compare a hardcover book to a mass-market book. The hardcover book will usually use acid-free paper, which will ensure its durability for many years. The mass-market book will use a lower-quality paper that will brown after a few years. Obviously, you get what you pay for, and this cost is reflected in the retail price of the book.

Price isn't the only consideration in paper choice. The production manager will also have to decide on the following.

- **Weight.** The weight of paper is determined by how much a standard ream of that particular paper weighs. For instance, 25 lb. paper means that a ream of 500 uncut sheets (25" × 38") of that paper weighs twenty-five pounds.
- **Bulk.** Bulk is determined by how many sheets of paper make up an inch.
- **Color and finish.** Color and finish affect the overall appearance of the pages.
- **Opacity.** This will determine if the text from the reverse page will show through.

As you can see, the paper alone calls for several decisions to be made. But the production manager's job does not end here. He will also have to decide on the type of binding for the book.

Binding

During the binding process, pages are put together in signatures, usually sewed or glued. A signature is a group of pages, normally thirty-two to a group. However, depending on the type of paper used, the press capabilities, and the trim size, a signature could also be sixteen, eight, or even four pages. The signatures are gathered and bound together, either by sewing or using an adhesive. The cover is then attached to the gathered signatures using an adhesive. If you don't understand this process, don't worry yourself about it. Just know that this is one of the many steps your book must go through to reach its final form.

FACT

A production manager may also have to locate and hire a company specifically for the binding. While some printers will have the capabilities for binding, not all do. A production manager will usually try to find a printer that can do it all, but if cost is a major consideration, she may not have that option.

Binding will affect how well the book opens. For instance, have you ever found yourself straining to keep a mass-market book open while reading? Sometimes it even requires two hands. Then again, the binding for music books often allows those books to open flat without your having to keep them open.

Going to Press

Once the production manager has made all necessary decisions, the book is ready to be sent to the printer. Because it is a minutely detailed and complex process, we will only briefly describe the printing process. Most authors find it interesting to learn at least the basics of what the book has to go through to reach its final form.

Blues

The printer will create a film from the files provided by the production manager. This film is used to create blueprints, commonly referred to as "blues." The blues represent the book's final form. They are bound pages, but the quality will not be as good as the final product. The blues will be the last chance the publisher has to review the book before it is sent to press. Corrections made at this stage are very costly. However, it is important to double check the placement of illustrations, make sure that all pages are there and in order, look for unwanted marks on the pages, and confirm that all elements have come together properly.

The editor will highlight any corrections that need to be made, then send the blues back to the printer. If there are several corrections, the book will need to be typeset again and pages adjusted, starting the process over. After corrections have been made, the book will go to press.

Print Run

The production manager specifies the quantity for the print run in the instructions to the printer. The print run is the approximate number of books to be printed. The film is then used to set up the press for the print run. The book will be printed on large sheets of paper, the paper will be folded and gathered into signatures, the signatures will be trimmed, and the book will be bound.

Four-Color Printing

If you have written a picture book that will be printed with full-color illustrations, there is an additional step to be aware of. While the printing process will remain the same, color will need to be added.

ESSENTIAL

Four-color printing will usually be used on covers if not in the book itself. The book jackets will go through a separate print run, and may even be printed at a different printing company. The jackets will normally be printed long before the book itself goes to the printer, since jackets are commonly needed in advance as sales materials.

This is usually done in a four-step process, hence the name four-color printing. The four colors used in this type of printing are cyan, magenta, yellow, and black (the four are commonly referred to as CMYK). The image will go through the printer four times, each time adding a new color. The combination of these four colors will result in the variety of different colors you find on covers, in magazines, and in illustrations.

The Bound Book

The production process, for an author trying to be so patient, can seem like a lifetime—especially since you will have little if any involvement. As you can see, the book goes through a lot of steps before reaching its final form. So if you were wondering why your book was scheduled to come out on a list two years after signing the contract, this is why.

Even after your book reaches the bound book stage, it will not immediately hit the bookshelves. The bound book will be shipped by the printer—or bindery if it was sent elsewhere to be bound—to the publishing company's warehouse. This trip could take anywhere from a couple of weeks to a couple of months, depending on how far the printer is from the warehouse.

A publishing company's warehouse may be down the street from the publisher, or in a different town or even a different state. This is where the books will be stored until they are sold to buyers. Large publishing companies may even have several warehouses scattered throughout the country.

Once the books arrive, inventory needs to be taken to ensure that the shipment is complete. The warehouse employees will then either get the go-ahead to begin processing orders or be told to hold the books for a while to give the reviewers time to do their thing and bring attention to the book. Advance copies may also be sent to potential buyers as a marketing strategy.

As the author, you will likely receive an advance copy as well. This will be your prized possession, at least until you get another book published! Editors realize how exciting this is for authors and normally don't waste much time getting the bound book in the mail. This advance copy is considered a courtesy, so don't expect your other free copies to be delivered just yet.

CHAPTER 17

Marketing and Publicity

You've spent a great deal of time trying to sell your manuscript to publishers, and at last you have succeeded. Congratulations! Now the real work begins. How is the publisher going to sell your book to the public? Remember that the success of your first book will have a bearing on your ability to publish more books down the road. It is crucial to work with your publisher on a comprehensive marketing and publicity plan, to give not just your book, but you as an author, a decent chance to thrive in the book business. This chapter will guide you through some of the common tactics used to help promote and sell your book.

The Catalog

The publisher's catalog is likely to be the first place your book receives any form of attention. Publishers normally have two lists per year—spring and fall—and a catalog to advertise each list. Your book will be categorized by the pub date, along with all other books coming out in the same month.

Either your acquisitions editor or a house publicist will write the catalog copy accompanying a picture of your book's cover, if one is ready in time. The book's announcement will also include trim size, page count, ISBN, author's bio, a brief description of the book including age or reading level, and price, and may mention any marketing plans intended for the book.

Sales reps will be busy trying to sell the books on an upcoming list and will bring a catalog along to their meetings. The catalog is a very useful selling tool, as it contains brief but succinct information that a book buyer can use to make a decision.

The sales team does not have time to sit down and read each book that they sell. Therefore, they will rely on information provided to them by editors and the catalog. The editors will likely have written up tip sheets, which include information about the book and the author (and illustrator, if applicable). The editor will then go before the sales team and give his own pitch for the books he represents. This gives the sales team an opportunity to get their questions answered and get a better feel for the books. Sometimes, they will receive other promotional materials to help back their sales pitches to buyers, but don't expect a whole lot for a first-time author. Normally, a spot in the catalog and a brief pitch from your editor is all the sales team is going to get for your book.

FACT

The catalog will present all the new titles for an upcoming list, as well as a few successful older titles. The new titles make up the publisher's frontlist, while the older ones are part of the backlist. This year your book is part of the frontlist; next year, your book could be part of the backlist.

The sales reps aren't the only ones who use the catalogs. A publicist may decide to send out catalogs to reviewers, journalists, and other such contacts to raise awareness and help promote the publisher's latest books. Interested book buyers may request a catalog if they haven't already been contacted by the sales reps. Individuals just like you, conducting research on a particular publisher, may also request a catalog to check out the upcoming titles.

FACT

The catalog will present all the new titles for an upcoming list, as well as a few successful older titles. The new titles make up the publisher's frontlist, while the older ones are part of the backlist. This year your book is part of the frontlist; next year, your book could be part of the backlist.

If you do not receive a catalog automatically, call or e-mail your editor and request one. This will probably be the first instance in which you see your name next to your book in print. It will be uplifting to see your book listing and to learn about the other titles sharing space in that season's catalog. You will find yourself in some very good company.

Book Reviews

Most publishing companies will send out review copies of new titles. Even though it costs publishers to mail out copies of books, the positive effect book reviews have on sales makes it well worth the price. Publishers want their books to be reviewed before the final pub date, in order to secure shelf space and media-generated buzz. Therefore, they will send out bound galleys for select titles. These are copies of the typeset book before it has been finished and sent to the printer. Other companies will wait for the book to be printed and send out advance copies before placing the book in stores.

QUESTION

What is a galley?
Before a book is made up into pages, the text is printed as a single column of type on long sheets of paper with wide margins for marking corrections. These sheets of text are called galleys. Sometimes they are sent out to reviewers, and sometimes they wind up in used bookshops. They can become collector's items.

A book review is great publicity and can heavily influence book buyers. Librarians, especially, will rely on book reviews to help make their decisions on what books to purchase for their library system. Reviews are great for public exposure, even if they are partially negative. Curious readers will buy a book they have seen reviewed in order to find out if they agree with the reviewer.

Making the Cut

A book review is a great way to bring your book to the attention of all book buyers, from the buyers for major chains to librarians to the general public, but getting your book reviewed isn't guaranteed. First you have to make the publisher's cut.

Because sending out books for review does cost money—when upwards of 500 copies are sent out, the price adds up quickly—publishers must decide which books are worth the investment. Some will decide to only send out titles they believe have the best shot at making it big. Some will send only those titles that have well-known authors' or illustrators' names attached to them. As a first-time author, your book may not make this initial cut.

ESSENTIAL

If you know of a specialized publication that may be interested in reviewing your book—such as a regional magazine or your local newspaper—let the publisher know. The publicist may not be aware of the publication, and its notice may be able to help you sell books. Editors and reporters often like to promote local writers.

Even if your book is sent to a high-profile reviewer, this doesn't guarantee a published review. Now that you've made the publisher's cut, you have to make the reviewer's cut, as well. Publications have only so much room for reviews and those come out only so often. Books that are chosen for reviews are often tied to a well-known name, whether it be author, illustrator, or publisher. While it seems as though it is exactly these that do not need the extra attention, they are what people want to read about.

On the bright side, there are a few publications that try to review all new books, giving each author a fair chance in this very competitive field. The next section will highlight some of these publications.

Where to Look for Reviews

Your book may not be placed in the hands of the *New York Times* book reviewer, but it will likely find its way via your publisher to at least one, if not all, of the following reviewers. These publications are those combed by industry professionals on a regular basis. A favorable review in one or more of these will almost certainly result in increased sales of your book. You are likely familiar with these publications from your market research. But now that you are published, you will be perusing them for a different purpose.

- *Booklist.* The American Library Association's magazine primarily targets librarians. The magazine reviews more than 2,500 children's books per year.
- *The Horn Book Guide.* A biannual publication that is dedicated to children's literature. It includes reviews on almost all new hardcover titles.
- *Publishers Weekly.* One of the major industry trade publications. Almost everyone involved in the book business reads it on a regular basis. It has a section devoted to reviews called "Forecasts," with a subsection for children's books. A starred review in PW will help get your book off and running.
- *School Library Journal.* This targets primarily librarians and boasts that it reviews more books per year than any other publication.

These publications aren't the only places you'll find reviews, but they are considered the major reviewers.

Evaluating Your Reviews

If your book does get a review, prepare yourself before reading it, and remember not to take any one review too much to heart. Reviewers have their own motivations—one may be attempting to set himself up as a brutally honest critic, and may have all but decided to rip your book apart before reading the first page. Another reviewer may be trying to establish herself as a writer in your area, and may feel threatened by your book. Although reviewers try to remain objective, many will be influenced to some extent by their own backgrounds, goals, and prejudices. Simply take each review with a grain of salt, and remember: All press is good press. The worst review will boost public exposure, and probably sales, for your book.

ALERT

Resist the urge to write a negative reviewer in anger. This will only serve to alienate that reviewer, which could backfire in the future. If you write to a journal to say a review was unfair, they will likely print your letter. But it will make you look like a whiner—unless you are pointing out a significant factual mistake.

On the other hand, if the review is favorable, now is the time to abandon your modesty. Clip it, frame it, show it to everyone you know. Put it up on your website! Above all else, take pride in the determination, sweat, and love that you put into your book, which led to this moment of someone appreciating it—in print.

Press Releases

The publicity department may write and send out press releases in addition to advance copies of your book. A press release is a sheet of information and advertising copy designed to generate interest in a book. Newspapers and magazines will often become interested in a book based on reading a press release, and will request an advance copy for review. This works out nicely for the publisher, who does not have to gamble the price of mailing out books before reviews are scheduled. Sometimes press releases are quoted in publications; but since press releases are basically advertisements, most magazine and newspaper editors do not feel comfortable using them as copy, and instead prefer to assess books independently and critically after reading them.

Some publishers will send press releases to all major newspapers throughout the country. Others will target only local areas or any area that has a relationship to the book, such as your hometown.

Media Tie-Ins

The press release will be brief and to the point. This is an introduction to your book and will include important general information such as title, author, type of book, and a brief description. Because it is used as a selling tool, the copy will try to grab the reader's attention from the start. While the press release may include pertinent information with only a few hooks thrown in here and there, publicists spend a lot of time brainstorming new angles from which to grab the attention of the media.

FACT

A publicist may also target specialized markets with press releases. So if you have written a book on sibling rivalry, a press release may be sent to parenting magazines or newsletters emphasizing the subject matter. If you can, suggest specialized newsletters, e-zines, or even blogs that might like to read the release and pass the word.

In the event that your book's subject ties in to a current media event, this is a perfect angle from which the press release copy may be written. For example, let's say you have written a book about a senator from your state, and then, just before the release of your book, that senator decides to run for president. Now, suddenly, the national spotlight is cast upon this senator, and the media is scrambling around, trying to gather as much information on him as possible. Lucky you!

To capitalize on this great stroke of luck, a savvy publicist will send out a press release promoting your book. You are one of the authorities on this senator, and all the major television networks will be calling you for an interview. Of course, luck has to be on your side to get this much of a media boost, but this example shows that press releases can grab the attention of the media if written from a creative angle and tied into current events.

Author Participation

The publicist has probably already asked you to fill out an author questionnaire, which asks for information the publicity department can use to help promote your book, such as where you currently live or where you grew up. If you haven't been asked to fill out a questionnaire, you may want to provide the publicity department with this information yourself.

If you know that your hometown newspaper or radio or TV station would be interested in doing a spotlight on a local author, give the publicist contact names and addresses. If you live in a small town, the publicist is unlikely to be familiar with local newspapers and magazines, and without your initiative, your book could miss out on valuable press opportunities. Try to think of any other publications that would be interested to learn about your book. Think of schools you graduated from, or organizations you belong to. Any of these may be ready and willing to help promote your book if given the chance. Collecting this information yourself makes it easier on the publicity department and increases your book's success.

Advertisements

The marketing department establishes marketing plans for all upcoming releases. The biggest ones might include author tours, full-page ads, posters, and promotional giveaways, but this isn't likely for first-time authors. While your book probably won't be singled out for a high-stakes marketing strategy, it may very well find itself among the list of other books featured in an advertisement.

Taking a Risk

Publishers take a risk when they buy ad space. Ads are expensive, and they are usually placed before the book hits stores, so the publisher does not know in advance how well the book is going to do, and whether they will get a return on their investment. Therefore, they must think long and hard about what route to take in advertising. In general, children's books do not have large marketing budgets, so using money to advertise one book (that may or may not sell well) will be taking money away from the other books on the list. However, publishers want to let book buyers know what they've got to offer, so they will sometimes take out one ad featuring a group of several titles. The money that would have been used for one book has now been used to promote several.

FACT

Ad space in a major trade publication could cost a publisher anywhere from several hundred to several thousand dollars. You may not have ads, but you can give interviews and library and school talks, and can publish short articles and reviews in your area of expertise to call attention to your book.

Group advertising promotes not only the upcoming books, but also the publisher. If several books are listed in one advertisement, this will show that the publisher is confident about *all* its books, not just one or two. Granted, there may not be room to give a description of your book, but wouldn't you rather see your book's title among the list of others with no description than to not have any advertising at all?

Of course, if your book is expected to sell big, it may get its very own space. Sometimes publishers will take out ad space in a consumer magazine that is specific to your book's topic. For instance, if you have written a nonfiction young adult book about eating disorders, the publisher may take out an advertisement in a magazine geared toward the health and fitness of teens, or maybe in a popular teen magazine's health section.

Co-op Advertising

Flipping through local newspapers or magazines, you may have come across an ad for a bookstore featuring a few select titles. Don't assume that if you can't get the desired advertising out of your publisher, you may be successful getting it out of a local bookstore. Those ads that you noticed are part of a cooperative (co-op) advertising agreement made between the publisher and bookstore.

In a co-op advertising agreement, the publisher agrees to divide the costs of an advertisement with a bookstore. However, the costs aren't normally divided up equally. The publisher usually ends up paying around 75 percent of the costs and the bookstore pays the remaining 25 percent. The ad will be taken out in the name of the bookstore with the bookstore's address and contact info, featuring the publisher's book.

ESSENTIAL

How many times have you walked through a major bookstore and found fantastic displays drawing you in to take a closer look at the books advertised? Did you know that the publisher pays the bookstore for the display space? Those displays may look personal, as if they were chosen by store employees, but they actually represent hard bargaining between publishing and bookstore executives.

For instance, if you are scheduled for a book signing in your hometown, the publisher may decide to advertise cooperatively with the bookstore in a local paper to raise awareness. Or a publisher could choose to pay co-op money for displays or posters advertising the upcoming book signing. While this may sound like a great idea, it isn't always the best option from the publisher's point of view.

Most small publishers do not participate in co-op advertising. The Federal Trade Commission states that any co-op advertising agreement made with one company must be made with any other company choosing to participate. In other words, if the publisher enters a co-op agreement consenting to pay 75 percent of a newspaper advertisement for one bookstore, the publisher is then obligated to pay 75 percent of a newspaper advertisement for any other bookstore that wants to participate. This can become very costly to small publishers that do not have huge advertising budgets for their books.

Conference Displays

Another common and important promotion your book may be considered for is its display at professional conferences. Publishing companies often attend several professional conferences a year. They will have a booth set up to display new releases and perhaps some strong-selling backlist titles. Representatives from the company will be there to work the booths, answer questions, and show off their products. Sometimes authors are invited by the publisher to attend and participate in book signings, though this is usually reserved for best-selling or top-name authors.

There are several conferences that take place throughout the year. You can check with *Publishers Weekly* (*www.publishersweekly.com*) to get a list of conferences and their dates. The two biggest conferences that you'll probably be interested in are the American Library Association's annual conference and BookExpo America (BEA). Both of these draw publishers from all over the country. Attendees can walk around and view the displays, talk to sales reps and editors, acquire an armload of free stuff, and make numerous contacts within the publishing industry.

If your book is displayed here, just think about all the people who will give it a glance, if not further study—authors, illustrators, librarians, booksellers, publishers, editors, sales reps, pretty much anyone involved in the book business. This is an important promotion for your book. Not only will it raise awareness of your book, it will also raise awareness of you as an author.

FACT

In addition to national conferences, publishers will attend international conferences at which they will set up exhibitions and try to sell foreign rights to their books. If your book is displayed here, you might just end up with a nice little chunk of money added to your royalty statement.

There are also smaller book fairs, conventions, and conferences that may be of interest to you. Check with your editor to see if the publisher will be setting up shop at any regional conferences. If you can attend, do so. It is an invaluable experience.

High-Profile Promotions

The most widely known marketing and publicity strategies include author tours, television and radio interviews, and advertised book signings. But don't start packing your bags just yet. These types of promotions are reserved for those authors and books that are top sellers for the company. Sure, if your book receives a literary award or makes it to the bestseller list, you'll have a good shot at your fifteen minutes of fame. However, most books and authors (though they may be top quality with solid selling records) do not reach this level of publicity, except in their local markets.

Publicists are not going to send review copies of your book to every talk show they can think of. This would waste time and money. Pay attention to books you hear about on talk shows. Have you already heard the author's name a thousand times before? Is the subject matter a hot topic in current events? Is the author or illustrator someone who's rich and famous? For most of the books you hear about, you will be able to answer yes to at least one of these questions.

High-profile promotions cost big bucks. This is why it isn't likely a publisher will choose to take such a risk on a first-time author. Unfortunately, fame is often a Catch-22 deal. No one will pay attention to you unless you are famous, and you can't become famous until someone gives you attention. Of course, there are always stories of overnight successes. You should hope—just don't bank on it.

ESSENTIAL

Don't rule out interviews completely. As an author, you do have something worthy of mention. You may still be able to get an interview with a local radio personality or newspaper reporter. Contact noon chat shows on both public and commercial radio stations in your area.

In case this chapter has left you feeling discouraged, let us end on a hopeful note. In today's evolving publishing world, much of the promotion you would like to see for your book is in your hands. The Internet has made it possible for writers to be their own publicists. The next chapter will discuss what you can do to promote your book and yourself. But before you commit yourself to launching a high-profile, high-stakes marketing plan, consider that perhaps an overnight smash hit is not really what you want. Remember, fame always carries a cost.

CHAPTER 18

Promoting Your Book Yourself

If you are like most writers, you will feel your book deserves more publicity and marketing than the publisher seems to provide. Perhaps you expected to participate in the effort yourself, with a book tour, including public readings and media interviews, yet you are surprised that your editor hasn't mentioned any of this. In addition, you may have read that today's authors must do more of their own book promotion than ever, and you may be anxious to start. So how do you begin?

Working with the Publisher

Before you begin your venture, find out exactly what the publisher is doing. Your acquisitions editor may have already filled you in on publicity and marketing plans for the book. Or it might be your developmental editor, or someone else in the publishing company, who is your main contact by the time your book is ready to emerge from the printer. Ask this person how the publisher plans to publicize and market your book.

Don't contact the publicist or the marketing manager on your own. The publisher will have a plan, and each team member will be busy carrying it out.

QUESTION

What is the difference between publicity and marketing?
Publicity is the promotion of a book for low cost and includes such things as book reviews, press releases, interviews, and your Internet presence. Marketing is the more expensive promotion of a book and includes such things as posters, displays, advertisements, and sales people who call on chain-store buyers.

You may be surprised to find that your publisher doesn't plan to ship many copies to bookstores. Your book will be featured in the publisher's fall or spring catalog, and because of that some bookstores will order it. But there may be no media blitz, and you may be disappointed to visit stores and search in vain for your title. Yet if the publisher's plan works, there will be a second phase of marketing.

After the hardcover's critical success, and after library sales cover publishing expenses, your book may come out as either a trade or a mass-market paperback. This is where the publisher hopes to make a profit. In paperback form your book may appear in stores, marketed to parents and grandparents who buy books for the children in their lives. But even in the paperback edition of your book, you may find that a national publicity and marketing campaign is only available to authors who are famous. Oh my goodness, you may think, this is my window of opportunity, and without more fanfare the book will be remaindered—sent back to the distributor with the cover torn off—before people have a chance to learn how good it is. What, you may well ask yourself, can I do to help?

Offering Your Services

It is important to ask your editor or other contact person whether they like to see authors give library readings, get radio and newspaper interviews, and visit schools to promote their books. Sometimes they want to coordinate such activities, but sometimes they leave you on your own. Each publishing company will have its own take on these issues, as will each editor. One of the deciding factors will be the way they perceive you: Will you be an effective presence to sell the book?

Your editor may help you establish working relationships with the publicist and marketing manager. They may ask for your ideas, so be prepared. If you know of print, broadcast, or web media that might be interested in your book, now is your chance to tell them. Your ideas will probably vary in cost and complexity, but all will require time and effort from the publisher's staff. Even if your idea is simply for a press release to be sent out to local newspapers, someone will have to research the newspapers' names and addresses, write and print the press releases, address and stuff the envelopes, and mail them off. Even the simplest ideas cost time and money.

Getting Involved in PR

One way to give your ideas a better shot is to do some of the work yourself. Using the example of suggesting a press release, you could research the names and addresses of those newspapers to which you want to send a press release and include a list with your idea. To go even further, you could write the press release yourself and send it along too. If some of the work is already done, this takes some of the load off of the publicity department and your idea will probably be looked upon more favorably. You may feel shy about writing promotional copy for your own book, but if you study the text that appears in ads for similar books, and on their back covers, then sit down and practice, you'll soon feel comfortable enough, and maybe even find it fun.

But what if your editor doesn't seem to want you to communicate with the publicity and marketing departments at all? In this case, hand over a list of your ideas, including addresses of media outlets and press releases, and politely wait for a response.

Creating an Online Presence

This is the best way to reach a great many potential readers of your book without leaving your house. No wonder writers have websites, blogs, and Facebook accounts! If you propose a book to a new agent or publisher, he will want to know what kind of presence you have on the Internet, and how many visits you receive there each month. Your web presence can have a big impact on sales of your book.

Creating a Website

If you visit the websites of your favorite authors, you will notice several things. They are nicely designed, with color schemes and photos, and they are organized with sections on the author's books or other creative products, reviews of those books, an author bio, teaching or workshop activities, and any services offered. These might include speaking engagements in schools, appearances in other venues, or the editing of manuscripts for fellow writers.

Your website presents you to the world. Remember that once text appears online, on a website, blog, forum, or in an email, it can quickly spread. Things can sometimes be removed from the site where they first appeared, but they will likely still exist in a server—a large computer that hosts sites—and they may reappear years later. So present yourself and your book online with grace, style, and care.

You may choose to work with a website designer, and you may want to interview several before making up your mind. Look at sites they've designed, and ask them to show you how to determine the rankings their websites have achieved on search engines, especially Google's search engine. Read *Getting Noticed on Google,* by Dustin Wax, or other books on search engine ranking. There is a lot to learn, but your designer/webmaster will help, and you can take it one step at a time.

Once your site is launched, it floats out there as your résumé, book publicity department, and offer of professional services. When you meet, in person or online, other writers for children, you can offer to exchange links. If you post someone's link on your site, and they post your link on their site, you will each draw readers from the other. This is a great way for writers to share audiences.

Creating a Blog

Whereas a personal website can be pricey, and is generally stable, blogs are typically cheap or free, and are dynamic. You can start one in a matter of minutes by signing up with WordPress, Blogger, or another company. You can post anything you desire, such as notices of your upcoming readings or school visits, reviews of other people's children's books, or reflections on your writing process. Remember that while it feels as if you are writing a letter to a friend, you are actually creating a permanent record for the planet. So think before you post, and edit carefully, twice.

A blog can function like a website that you directly control, which can be useful and fun. Some people use them as journals of their every thought and trip to the grocery. With care and restraint, you may be able to sustain a conversation that will interest potential customers for your books. It's a unique venue for writers—part private journal, part social conversation with friends, and part marketing device to interest strangers in your work. Read a number of blogs by writers you admire before you take the plunge.

Creating a Facebook Account

Welcome to social media! Many people already have a Facebook account to post photos and keep up with friends and colleagues. But did you know the site can also be a great tool for self-promotion? With its free membership and ease of use, Facebook can be one of the most accessible and helpful publicity venues available to writers. You can use your personal Facebook page to publicize your books and writerly activities, or you can start a second account specifically for the promotion of your books.

The trick is balance—no one wants to receive constant updates from their "friends" that are truly nothing more than mini press releases. So rather than blasting your friends and family with promotional information, start by establishing friends in the realm of children's book publishing, such as writer friends. This way, you can gradually develop a wide network of people who share your interests.

Keep the tone light and social, but keep in mind your purpose of networking for the sake of your books. This is the idea of "social networking"—something of a contradiction. "Social" implies authentic, heartfelt connections, while "networking" implies business connections. You need to find a balance: don't be too informal and silly, and don't be too hard-sell. Keep in mind that you are not writing a private letter or journal—you are adding to your permanent record. Allow cordial but focused notes to and from people who love children's books, and use the site as a tool to expand your personal network of contacts in the children's book world.

ESSENTIAL

Add to your image as a children's writing professional using Facebook photo albums. Post pictures of that book conference you attended, or your writing room, or yourself in a classroom with children. Avoid posting photos that may detract from this image (such as pictures containing alcohol).

LinkedIn

LinkedIn is a professional social networking site emphasizing business relationships. Membership is free, and you list your background, skills, and the type of work you are seeking. Connect with former colleagues and old friends now working in various professional fields.

FACT

Wikipedia's List of Social Networking Sites lists about 200 sites and includes the rules for membership and the number of people signed up for each. Take some time and explore, and you'll probably find several sites that fit your interests.

Goodreads

Goodreads is a site for sharing the latest books you've read with friends. Many teachers and children's authors enjoy posting short notices about their reading each week, so this is a good way to discover new writers, as well as to make connections with people who will take an interest in your books.

Book Publicity the Old-Fashioned Way

You may feel a bit overwhelmed by all these ways to use the Internet. What about visiting bookstores, and giving interviews to newspapers, the way writers used to publicize their books? Those activities can still work for you. If you don't like dealing with technology, there is a compromise that can give you the best of both worlds. Establish a website, but don't change it frequently. Go out and do some school and library visits, talk to bookstore managers about readings, and get the feel of meeting people face-to-face over your book. By trying all these avenues you'll discover the ones you're good at and the ones you enjoy.

Visiting Bookstores

While you are working on your book, start becoming friendly with the staff at bookstores in your area. Attend local author readings and book signings, and make yourself part of the local literary culture. When your book comes out, your relationships with these bookstores may help put your book on the shelves. Also, do some research into the booksellers in nearby cities—drive over, check them out, get friendly with the staff and attend their events from time to time. Eventually, these connections will come in handy and assist your efforts to publicize your finished book.

Introducing Yourself

When your book comes out, and you are ready to approach a bookstore where no one knows you, first find out if the store has your book in stock. If not, you may want to have a friend or two or several order the book to raise interest. If the book is in stock, be friendly and chat a little with the staff. Introduce yourself and your book. You may find that the staff will open up with information regarding how well your book is selling. However, don't interrogate the staff. If you flat out ask if your book is selling well, this will put the employee on the spot. Maybe he has never even seen your book. Having to admit such a thing will likely make a person feel uncomfortable and want to escape the conversation as soon as possible. Your best bet is to always assume no one knows you or your book.

Becoming chummy with a bookseller may entice her to give a little attention to your book, especially if the bookstore is an independent, located in your area. This isn't likely to happen with the chain superstores—they expect to be paid for any attention given to a book. However, if you have a cozy independent children's bookstore in your local area, the store manager may very well choose to display your book for a short period, announcing you as a local author.

Book Events

If you want to promote your book with an event, such as a book signing, you must first verify that the particular bookstore actually holds such events. Some bookstores only sell books and do not bother with hosting public events. Call the bookstore and ask. Any employee should be able to tell you.

ESSENTIAL

If you are scheduled to participate in a book event, let your editor know in advance. She may decide to advertise the event locally or at least ensure that extra copies of your book make it to the bookstore in time for the event.

Visit the bookstore and request a copy of its calendar of events. This will tell you what type of events normally take place and give you an idea of how far in advance the bookstore schedules these events. For instance, if the calendar lists events for the next three months, you can bet that you will have to schedule at least three months in advance. Next you will need to decide what type of event you would like to see take place. This could be anything from a book signing to an author reading to a character party where the kids dress up in costumes pertaining to the book.

Contacting the Right Person

To pitch your idea for an event, begin by contacting either the store manager or the person in charge of community relations. When you find out who is the appropriate person to speak with, try to speak with that person directly. You may even want to send an e-mail introducing yourself and describing your idea for the event. Be sure to include the title and ISBN for your book! Attach your press release to the e-mail.

If you are a first-time author, you may find that the bookstore isn't interested in scheduling your event. Don't worry too much about this. Thank the person you spoke to for her time and move on to the next bookstore on your list. The first bookstore may have actually done you a small favor. Think about it: If you are an unknown and you schedule a book signing, you may be gravely disappointed to see only two people show up the whole day (aside from the friends who came out of obligation). This happens to everyone, so be prepared. If a single person shows up to discuss your book, put as much energy into discussing your work, and answering questions, as if you had twenty people.

If the bookstore doesn't wish to schedule you for an event, or if it doesn't sponsor events at all, you can still promote your book. Offer to sign the copies of your book the store has in stock. Sometimes bookstores set up bins especially for autographed books. Even if they don't, an autograph may persuade someone to buy your book.

Visiting Libraries

Libraries are an important promotional venue. Often children find great books in the library, only to later pester their parents into buying them. And word of mouth can work wonders for the overall sales of a book. Promotion is not just selling; it is also raising awareness and getting your book out there.

Visit your local library. First see if it even owns a copy of your book. If not, don't stress out, but you may want to donate a copy. The library will be glad to have it and may even place it face out on the shelf or set it out on a display table. Librarians want to bring in people just as much as bookstores do. If they believe a local author, such as you, will help get the public's attention, they will use your book as a hook.

Introduce yourself to the children's librarian as a local author. Offer to sign a copy of your book for the library to keep. Be friendly and polite. Let the librarian know that you are available for any type of event that would showcase your book. Often librarians like to have authors (or anyone!) during the after-school hour to read to children, or to discuss a book. Don't be pushy, but listen carefully to the kinds of events the library favors. Just make a good impression and don't overstay. Build your relationship for the future. Remember, you want to be perceived as a slightly mysterious, busy, and talented writer, who would be willing to share some of your time with children.

Getting Help from Friends

Your friends can join the publicity campaign in a variety of ways. Get creative with your schemes, and ask their advice as well. Two heads are certainly better than one in this case. Maybe your book would lend itself to a character- or holiday-themed dress-up party. Perhaps you could do this as a birthday party for a friend's child.

FACT

While you should certainly visit your hometown library, don't let this be your only library effort. Call and e-mail libraries in nearby towns and cities, as well as school libraries. Call the schools, ask for the contact person, send her an e-mail note with the press kit, then call back in a week to follow up.

Targeting Bookstores

If you have willing friends in various locations around the country, ask them to visit their local bookstores to see if your book is in stock. If it isn't, ask your friend to order a copy. Of course, he will have to pick it up and pay for it—ordering the book and then returning it won't help your cause. This may entice a bookstore to keep a copy of your book in stock. If there are any children's bookstores where your friends live, these should definitely be visited.

One tactic editors and authors alike sometimes employ is to visit bookstores and turn their books face out. A book's jacket or cover will likely catch a customer's wandering eye and just might entice her to pick up the book and learn more about it.

Public Speaking

Some writers are not comfortable talking in public; others are but prefer not to. There is no shame in this. After all, one reason you write is to work alone and use your creativity slowly and carefully. Solitary work is a great thing, with a spiritual dimension.

On the other hand, many people would enjoy some public exposure for the sake of their work but have a fear of public speaking or have little or no experience. They just need to take baby steps and practice. First, try reading a chapter or two in front of a mirror. This will teach you valuable lessons, such as how many minutes it takes to read a few pages, and how to pace your reading to be clear and dramatic. Once you have become comfortable reading in private, practice on family members or friends and ask for their feedback.

There is great promotional value in promoting your book before an audience. Even if you don't make the effort yourself, some day soon you might be asked for a radio interview, or asked to be on a panel at a conference or to read in a library or bookstore. You don't want to go into such a situation cold. Get your practice in now, so you can take advantage of opportunities in the future.

Interviews

Let's say you're ready and willing to grab any opportunity to speak about your book, but your publisher hasn't set up any interviews. This doesn't mean you should rule them out. With a little work, you could get a short spot on a local radio or television station to promote your book. Before you run to the phone to set up an interview, you will need to come up with a hook and put together a press kit.

If you want to get an interviewer's attention and persuade him to feature your book, you'll have to give that person something to work with. As mentioned earlier, if your book can be tied into some current event, this is great. Be sure to emphasize this in your press kit. If you can't tie it to a current event, try to dig up some new statistics about your topic. You will need to approach this from an angle that highlights the relevance of your book. Get creative and brainstorm.

ESSENTIAL

If you have set up your own interviews, don't expect your publisher to pay for your expenses while traveling. Unless you are an author of a bestseller, it isn't likely that the publisher has budgeted for such expenses. However, do let your contact person at the publisher know about your scheduled interviews. She may decide to send out press releases or spring for a local ad.

Putting Together a Press Kit

A press kit should at the very least contain an author bio, a press release, and sample questions for the interview. If you have supplied any of these materials to the publisher, you already have part of your press kit started. If your book has received favorable reviews, include copies of these, too, and if you have scheduled a book event, mention this as well. Include anything you feel would add to your book's importance.

Send your press kit off to local media outlets. Because you are a local author, you are likely to get at least a little bit of attention. If you plan on spending time elsewhere, target the stations in that area as well. Be sure to include your dates of availability.

Speaking at Schools

If you are interested in promoting your book to a group of children, or in some cases teenagers, speaking in schools may appeal to you. Your speech could take many forms, and will take a lot of thought. Because you are speaking directly to children, you will have to capture their interest and attention from the get-go. You will have to make it fun, exciting, interesting, and informative all at the same time. The pay for these types of visits varies from author to author, and place to place. You may be able to get an idea of the average fee in your area by doing an Internet search, or by asking a teacher.

Think of the events you considered proposing to a library or bookstore. Some of these may also work in a school setting, but you will have to decide whether presenting your book to a smaller or larger group is preferable. For instance, if you have written a picture book, you may want to animate your characters through the use of your voice or even act out parts of the story to keep your young audience's attention. This would probably work better in a classroom setting than in a large auditorium.

If your book is for older children, you may want to read a portion of it aloud to them and discuss the writing process. You could add in activities that pertain to the story, or give the children short and fun assignments that demonstrate a stage in the writing process. However, be careful that you don't actually use the word *assignment,* or the children may turn off to the idea. You want this to be a fun experience that covers up the fact that they are actually learning something.

If you are interested in speaking in schools, the best place to start is with your local school system. Call and speak to the principal. Give a brief description of your idea and see if she is interested. If so, you can follow up with your author bio, a copy of the book, or parts of your press kit—something that will give the principal an idea of what you will be presenting. From there you can work with the principal to schedule a date and time, and determine the setting and audience. Once you have a date, communicate with the teacher or other contact person. Perhaps you could send him a copy of your book, or fax or e-mail him a chapter. If the students have time to read a little of your work, they will be much more interested. They will look forward to asking you questions about your research and writing process. Discuss in detail what you will do, and ask the teacher for suggestions. Have your visit planned down to the exact minute. Schools run on bells and buzzers; you'll be surprised at how precisely your session will begin and end.

Go the Extra Mile

Of course, you could do all of this and still want to do more. This is where your creative genius comes into play. Brainstorm all possible ways for your book to gain attention. Start with those that aren't so over the top and go from there. Be careful that you don't become so zealous that you drain your bank account. Some promotion strategies can make quite a dent in your checkbook. Consider low-cost approaches to self-promotion, such as fliers you can create for free on your computer and post on bulletin boards in libraries, schools, or community centers.

Traditionally, it is not appropriate for authors to sell their own books. Your contract may restrict you from doing so anyway. But there are exceptions. You may be invited to appear at a school, on a panel, in a church, in a library, or other venue, where the invitation includes the suggestion that you bring books to sell. If your publisher permits you to buy a box of books at the wholesale price, maybe a friend or friends would come with you and set up a little "shop" at the venue. Be sure that whoever is doing the actual selling is able to make change, and keep records for your taxes. Have a clipboard with a sign-up sheet for fans who would like to give you their names and e-mail addresses, so you can inform them of future books and events.

ALERT

Don't get so caught up in your promotion campaign that you forget to write. After all, if your first book is a success, your fans will be impatiently waiting for another. If you have a website, you can spend most of your time researching and writing your books and a few minutes every month or two updating your fans.

Book promotion is an interesting experience. You might be good at doing it on the Internet, but uncomfortable handling events in public. Or you might love appearing in schools (and collecting the fees), but find web marketing tedious. Try both approaches, because anything you do will probably lead to new contacts, skills, experiences, and opportunities. But don't give book promotion too big a role in your life. Spend most of your work time thinking, researching, writing, and revising. If you write a good book and have a little luck, your audience will find it.

CHAPTER 19

Grants and Awards

Throughout this book, you've read over and over how difficult writing and getting published can be. Well, now it's time to put the difficulties aside and focus on what that hard work can do for you. This chapter will introduce you to the awards and recognition you may receive as a children's writer, as well as let you in on the joys of grant money.

Financial Aid

Did you know that there are grants available to help you establish a writing career? We're not talking about the royalties or flat fees your publisher is contracted to pay you upon publication. Private estates and corporations, as well as many state and federal arts councils, set aside a certain amount of money each year for writers' grants. This money is given out to individuals or groups for aid in working toward a specific purpose, in this case children's literature. Grants must be applied for, which can sometimes be a grueling process, but once awarded, grant money does not have to be paid back.

There are many different types of grants available for both emerging and established writers. Some are available only for specific genres, while others are open to all genres. Some offer a few hundred dollars and some offer several thousand. Some cover only specific expenses, such as books or writing supplies, and others can be used for any expense related to your writing needs, from child-care to rent.

ESSENTIAL

In addition to applying for grants, you can also submit your work to contests. Hundreds of contests are conducted every year, covering all genres. Normally, there is a monetary award given to the winners and runners-up. However, you should beware of scams. Do an Internet search with the words "writing contest scams" to learn the signs.

You are likely to find one or several grants that you are qualified for and that suit your writing needs, but pursuing them is a task unto itself. All too often, writers are either unaware of grant opportunities, fail to do the research needed to find the right grants, or assume they won't get the grant and simply don't try for it. Because of this, a lot of money is out there for the taking and only a small pool of enterprising writers are being considered for it. Never be afraid to apply. Even if you don't get the grant, you will learn from the process, and at the next opportunity you will be less afraid to take action.

Where to Look

If you are interested in researching grants, you can begin with checking the websites of the writers' organizations you belong to. For instance, the Society of Children's Book Writers and Illustrators offers a number of grants to members, including $2,000 Work-in-Progress grants for distinct categories, such as unpublished novelists or nonfiction writers, or those whose writing features minority perspectives. Numerous writers' organizations out there offer grants to a wide spectrum of entrants; in most cases, everything you need to know about locating and applying for these grants is detailed on the organizations' websites. After researching groups of which you are a member, move on to consider others. Even if you don't secure grant money from one of these organizations, you may happen upon a group you hadn't heard of before and choose to become a member, which could lead to any number of opportunities down the road.

Your next stop should be an online search focused on locating grant money for writers. The Internet is a huge, constantly evolving, minimally regulated place, and as such it contains a lot of worthwhile information and a lot of trash. Be skeptical of sites offering to apply for grants on your behalf for a (large) fee, or those advertising grants that are expensive to apply for. Sign up for the e-mail newsletter put out by Funds for Writers (*www.fundsforwriters .com*), which scans the web for new grants and updates regularly.

Next, try your local library. Search its database for books offering grants for children's writing, but don't stop there. You may also be qualified for grants outside the specifics of children's writing. For instance, you could be eligible for grants awarded to West Coast writers or those working within a specific area, such as AIDS awareness. If you have the time and energy, look through all books on grants that the library has to offer.

How to Apply

Applying for grants is a tedious undertaking. You will need to contact the organization sponsoring the grant for qualifications, guidelines, and application forms. You will usually need to prepare samples of your work to include in the submission. Though it may not sound too difficult (you fill out applications and forms all the time, right?), applying for a grant actually requires a very specific form of writing.

The most important thing to remember is to follow the directions to a T. If the application directs applicants to print their names and phone numbers on every page of writing samples, do it—if not, your application will likely be tossed out, unread. This may sound harsh, but consider the pressures grant-awarding boards are under. They have to sift through thousands of files to select the most deserving applicants from the pile. Naturally they are going to want to offer the grant money to people who have taken the application seriously. In most cases, applicants who ignore the small rules have been sloppy with other aspects of their applications, too. So follow directions: take it upon yourself to make sure your application at least gets read.

FACT

There are several organizations and service firms that will help you with the grant writing process for a fee. If you choose to take this route, be sure to research the organizations and shop around. Fees and qualifications vary.

Your best bet is to research grant writing before diving into it on your own. Though there are writers out there who never apply for grants, there are also those who tap into these opportunities on a regular basis and are familiar with the proper procedures. To have a fighting chance against these individuals, your grant-writing skills need to be top-notch. There are several books and guides available that will help you learn the art of grant writing, such as *Finding Funding: The Comprehensive Guide to Grant Writing* by Daniel M. Barber. A number of these will likely be found in your local library.

The Newbery Medal

So you still have dreams of fame and fortune? Well, you just might get both of them if you are awarded the Newbery Medal. The Newbery Medal is considered the highest honor a children's book author can receive. Everyone in the world of children's literature waits eagerly every year for the announcement of the winner.

Winning the Newbery Medal will put your name on the lips of all involved in the industry. Recognition isn't the only reward, though. You will also see a tremendous boost in the sales of your book, since every library, bookseller, and many children and adults will suddenly feel the need to own your book. The Newbery Award places a permanent stamp of excellence and respect not only upon its winners, but also upon those it designates as Newbery Honor Books.

History of the Medal

John Newbery was the eighteenth-century bookseller who was responsible for the turning point in children's literature with the publication of *A Little Pretty Pocket-Book*. This book combined elements of education and instruction with amusement and entertainment, paving the way for modern children's books. Publisher Frederic G. Melcher recognized Newbery's achievement and in 1921 proposed to the American Library Association (ALA) that an award be presented in his honor. The ALA readily agreed, and thus the first children's book award was born. Ever since then, the Association for Library Service to Children, a division of the ALA, awards the Newbery Medal annually to one children's book author.

FACT

The winner of the Newbery Medal receives a bronze medal that was designed by René Paul Chambellan in 1921. The winner's name and date are engraved on the back of the medal.

As the first and most distinguished children's book award in the world, the Newbery Medal carries a lot of weight. The medal's purpose, according to the ALA, is "to encourage original creative work in the field of books for children. To emphasize to the public that contributions to the literature for children deserve similar recognition to poetry, plays, or novels." The Newbery Medal has certainly lived up to its purpose.

Qualifications and Criteria

Since only one author can win this award per year, there must be qualifications set to help make the difficult decision a bit easier. Those children's books considered must have been published the previous year and authored by a U.S. citizen or resident. The book must also have been published in the United States. Reprints and compilations are not eligible. The book's target audience must be any age group of children through the age of fourteen.

The book can consist of any type of writing (fiction, nonfiction, poetry), and the text is primarily what will be taken into consideration. The book must make what the judges deem the most "distinguished contribution to American Children's Literature" of all children's books published that year in America in English. The committee can't take into consideration an author's past works or the author's reputation, nor can the committee take into account how well the book sells or its popularity. The book can't rely on other media and must be a "self-contained entity."

When deciding on a book's degree of excellence, the committee must take into consideration the interpretation of the theme or concept, the handling of characters and setting, how the plot is developed, overall presentation and organization, and style.

Finding excellence in children's literature is easy; deciding on the "most distinguished American children's book" is not. This was understood from the very beginning, and so the committee is allowed to recognize other books for their merit. These books are called Newbery Honor Books.

The Caldecott Medal

It was a wonderful day back in 1921 when the Newbery Medal was founded, because the authors of children's books were finally getting the recognition they deserved. This continued happily until people began to realize that several books reached their quality of excellence through the illustrations. But the illustrators weren't getting the credit they deserved.

History of the Medal

In 1937, Frederic G. Melcher again went before the American Library Association and proposed that another award be established to honor the artist who created "the most distinguished picture book of the year." This honor would be called the Caldecott Medal, named after the nineteenth-century English illustrator Randolph J. Caldecott. Of course, the board loved the idea.

Every year since, the Association for Library Service to Children has awarded the Caldecott Medal to one illustrator alongside the presentation of the Newbery Medal. These two medals go hand in hand in recognition and stature.

FACT

The winner of the Caldecott Medal also receives a bronze medal that, just like the Newbery Medal, was designed by René Paul Chambellan, though it was created later, in 1937. The winner's name and date are engraved on the back of the medal.

Qualifications and Criteria

This medal, too, has qualifications and criteria that must be met for a book to be considered. Since this medal is also hosted by the ALA, the criteria are quite similar to those for the Newbery Medal.

The book must have been published in the United States during the previous year and illustrated by a U.S. citizen or resident. The illustrations must be original work and found in no other source. The book's target audience must be children. Though most picture books are targeted to younger children, the age of the target audience may be through age fourteen. The illustrations must provide a child with a "visual experience," in which the story line or concept is developed through the series of illustrations.

ESSENTIAL

Though the Caldecott Medal is given to artists only, should your book receive the award, take a little bit of credit yourself. While the illustrator is certainly a genius in his own right, remember that it is your words that gave the artist the inspiration needed to create the winning illustrations.

The committee can't take into consideration an illustrator's past works or the illustrator's reputation, nor can the committee take into account how well the book sells or its popularity. The book can't rely on other media and must be a "self-contained entity." Committee members make their decision based primarily on the illustrations, though other elements (such as the text) can be taken into consideration.

The committee must take into consideration the illustrator's execution of the artistic technique chosen, how well the illustrations act as an interpretation of the text, how well the style complements the story line or concept, the use of illustration to describe characters and setting, and/or the use of illustration to convey information.

Of course, there are hundreds of excellent illustrators out there. Because only one can be honored with the Caldecott Medal each year, the committee is also allowed to select the work of other artists to be commended as Caldecott Honor Books.

National Awards

The Newbery and Caldecott Medals are the most coveted awards for children's literature, but they aren't the only distinguished awards given. There are several other national awards given out annually to notable children's writers. This section will highlight some of the better-known awards.

Coretta Scott King Award

The Coretta Scott King Award is sponsored by the American Library Association and honors both Dr. Martin Luther King, Jr. and his wife for their efforts to promote peace. This annual award is presented to an African-American author and African-American illustrator who create quality children's literature promoting cultural values and the understanding and acceptance of all people.

Margaret A. Edwards Award

The Margaret A. Edwards Award for Outstanding Literature for Young Adults is sponsored by *School Library Journal* and awarded by the Young Adult Services Library Association. The award honors an author for lifetime achievement in writing for teenagers. The winner's books focus on helping teenagers to understand themselves and their relationship to society.

Laura Ingalls Wilder Medal

This award is presented by the Association for Library Service to Children to an author or illustrator whose body of work provides a significant and lasting contribution to children's literature. (The books must have been published in the United States.) Originally presented every five years, the award is now presented every three years. The award honors Laura Ingalls Wilder, author of books including *The Little House in the Big Woods*.

National Book Award

The National Book Award for Young People's Literature is the National Book Foundation's award for quality children's literature. Established in 1950, the National Book Award is a prestigious and well-known honor. Every year in November the awards are presented in four categories: fiction, nonfiction, poetry, and young people's literature. The winner of each category receives not only recognition and honor but also a $10,000 cash award. Consideration for children's literature is open to U.S. authors of all genres.

The *Boston Globe*–Horn Book Award

This award is sponsored by the *Boston Globe* and Horn Book, Inc. Submissions are sent in by U.S. publishers, but the author does not have to be a U.S. citizen. Submissions are evaluated and winners are selected by a committee of three professionals from the children's publishing industry. Awards are presented annually at the New England Library Association conference in three categories: picture book, fiction, and nonfiction.

The Golden Kite Award

The Golden Kite Award is sponsored by the Society of Children's Book Writers and Illustrators. Submissions are open only to members of the society. Unlike other national awards, the winner of the Golden Kite Award is determined by other authors and illustrators. Three members of the children's writing committee are chosen to judge nominations for each category. The award is given in four categories: fiction, nonfiction, picture book text, and illustration.

Orbis Pictus Award

The Orbis Pictus Award is presented by the National Council of Teachers of English to an author who has created a quality work of children's nonfiction published in the United States. The award honors Johann Comenius, the author of *Orbis Pictus—The World in Pictures*, published in 1658, which is considered the first informative book actually designed and written specifically for children.

State Awards

In addition to the national awards, several states give out their own awards. For some awards, the winner is determined by the votes from children statewide, which not only encourages children to read but also asks them to form and state their opinions about those books they read, opening up literary discussions. In this way, awards benefit not just the author but also those children who participate in the award process. Other State awards are determined by committees of teachers and/or librarians.

This section highlights some state awards to give you an idea of what is out there. However, these are not the only ones available. Nearly every state grants its own award and several give out multiple awards. Those books awarded in a particular state will see an increase in sales to libraries in that state.

- **Kentucky Bluegrass Award.** The books can be nominated by any adult, although most nominations come from librarians, publishers, and teachers. The winners are chosen by the children of Kentucky schools. Awards are given according to grade category: kindergarten through second, third through fifth, sixth through eighth, and ninth through twelfth.
- **Rebecca Caudill Young Readers' Book Award.** Named for historical children's writer Rebecca Caudill, this award is given once a year to the author of an outstanding work of children's literature, as voted by the children of Illinois school, grades four through eight.
- **Louisiana Young Readers' Choice Award.** Each year, fifteen books are selected by a committee of school and public librarians across the

state of Louisiana and sent to schools for students to vote on. Two awards are given, one for grades three through five and another for grades six through eight. Honor books in both age groups are also named.

- **Black-Eyed Susan Book Award.** Students in the state of Maryland vote for winners in four categories: picture books, books for grades four through six, books for grades six through nine, and books for high school students.
- **Patricia Gallagher Picture Book Award.** The Oregon Reading Association honors one outstanding book per year featuring text and illustrations. Children of all ages are invited to participate in the voting process.
- **Prairie Pasque Award.** Sponsored by the South Dakota Library Association, this award's winners are determined by the number of votes received from South Dakota students in grades three, four, and five. Nominations are made by a committee of librarians and teachers.

These awards represent only a small number of those offered. Young adult novel author Cynthia Leitich Smith keeps an updated list of state writing awards for children's and young adult authors, with links to each state's contest website, at her blog, *www.cynthialeitichsmith.com.*

ESSENTIAL

While most state awards are not as well-known as the national awards, many writers find that winning a state award is a most valued honor. Because many state awards are granted on the basis of children's votes, this means that it is your intended audience praising your work, and not just a committee of adults.

Honorable Mention

While winning an award is a surefire way to gain recognition as a distinguished writer, it isn't the only way. There are several associations and organizations that compile lists of recommended books. Some are better known than others, but if you are included on any of these lists, you will add valuable credit to your name.

Children's Choices

The International Reading Association and the Children's Book Council have teamed up to sponsor the Children's Choices list of children's books (see *www.reading.org*). Unlike other lists that highlight the books adults think are best for children, this list contains books that are voted on by the children themselves. If you are interested in hearing what your targeted audience has to say about the literature they are currently reading, you should check out this list. The list of Children's Choices is divided into three categories: beginning and young readers, intermediate readers, and advanced readers.

Every year, children from all over the country read those books submitted by publishers and vote for their favorites. A list of approximately 100 titles is compiled and published for booksellers, parents, librarians, authors, publishers, and children to see just what has made it into the hearts and minds of the intended audience. If your book happens to show up on this list, take great pride in your work. You have been selected by those who matter most—the children.

ALA Notables

In addition to the Newbery Medal and Honor Books and the Caldecott Medal and Honor Books, the American Library Association compiles an annual list of Notable Children's Books. The ALA encourages libraries to make these books available to children, so if your book shows up on this list, you may see an increase in library sales.

Oprah's Book Club Kids Reading List

All writers are aware of what a recommendation from Oprah can do for the sales of a book. While most people think Oprah recommends only adult books, she does also make a reading list of children's books. Oprah's Book Club Kids Reading List is divided into age groups: infant to two years, three to five years, six to nine years, nine to twelve years, and twelve years and older. You can find this list at *www.oprah.com/packages/kid-reading-list*.

Best Books of the Year

Several industry publications create their own lists of quality children's books every year. For instance, the editors of *School Library Journal* select a number of outstanding books to include in their list, Best Books. Editors at *Publishers Weekly* compile an annual list of what they consider "the year's most distinguished titles" in Best Children's Books. *Booklist* has its own ideas of what books are outstanding and showcases them in its annual list of Editors' Choice, which is divided into categories for young readers, middle readers, older readers, and young adults.

Though just a few lists are mentioned here, there are more out there. Publishers, teachers, parents, associations, librarians, and children all have their own lists of children's books that are the best. Reading about all these awards, and especially the criteria used in judging, should give you the sense of a large community of thoughtful people who care deeply about the quality of children's books. They are doing all they can to encourage you— not only to write, but to tackle subjects that matter most to children, and to write the best books you can.

CHAPTER 20

Where Will You Go from Here?

Whether you've just completed your first manuscript or have had several books published already, you are faced with the decision of what to do next. Some writers dislike actually writing, but like *having written*. Many others love the creative process, including seeking new experiences, gathering ideas, researching, outlining, composing, and revising. Whether you prefer the process or the product, you'll want to keep writing, every day.

Keep Writing

There are some excellent guides offering tips for writing. They provide different insights into the craft, but they all agree on one thing: If you continue to write, your process will become easier, and your work will improve.

Regardless of whether you are currently searching for a publisher, conducting research, trying a narrative strategy, or working a job to pay bills, you should write every day. Give yourself a schedule, and establish goals. What if you have a day job and a family? You may only get one or two hours a day for your writing, but if your goal is to get published, you must hold to your schedule.

Write at the same time, in a quiet and private place (or the right coffee shop), and your brain will become used to opening the doors of creativity at that time. Give yourself a fixed number of hours to read books like those you want to write, and a fixed number of hours for research into your ideas. Don't forget the actual writing hours!

ESSENTIAL

Your writing life itself is a creative process. Honor it by working steadily and joyfully. Keep a balance between short- and long-term goals, and between writing that focuses on your past experiences and that which tackles new experiences. Determine to tell the stories that have shaped you, and the ones you will live in the future.

Looking Ahead

If you have a manuscript in the editorial or production phase of publication, then begin a new project. Not only will it help keep your mind off of what is happening to your manuscript, but it will also give you something to talk about when your editor asks about any other work you have to show. If an editor is interested in building a relationship with you, the last thing you want to do is come up empty-handed. Be ready with a quick idea pitch, and if that one is batted down, be ready with another. If the editor is intrigued, be prepared to present your proposal in greater depth.

If you are having difficulty coming up with a new idea that's as good as your first one, you will need new inspiration. Spend a few hours wandering in the stacks of a good library. Look at old books, and books in various fields. Keep a notebook in your hand, and let the ideas flow to you. Don't worry about putting pen to paper just yet. By reading and taking notes you are storing up material and preparing for the next writing phase. Remember that much of your writing comes from your subconscious mind, "from where you dream," in Robert Olen Butler's phrase, the title of his book on fiction writing. Don't try to force your creativity, just keep to your schedule, makes notes to yourself, and catch glimpses of ideas as they emerge.

Post-Publication

Getting that first book published is every writer's goal. If you have already published a book, you will want to publish a second (as well as a third and fourth) book. But what if that first book hasn't sold very well, for whatever reason? Your publisher may not want to sign you up for anything else. Does that mean you're a failure? Of course not. It just means your publisher isn't willing to go the distance and you will have to search for another one that will.

Most writers need to find a new publisher at some point. Strive to make your second book better than the first. You have to prove to future publishers that you are an excellent writer, regardless of the first book's sales figures.

Now let's say your book was a top seller for the publishing company. While you may think it gets easier from here, the opposite is actually true. Your readers liked what they saw in the first book; now you have to keep their favor with the second. This means that the second book has to be just as good as, if not better than, the first or you risk losing your audience for any future books you write.

The more success you have, the higher the expectations publishers and readers will have for your future books. Think of how this works with musicians and actors and painters. If they depart from their popular work, audiences may resist their efforts. Yet if they are to remain creative they must try new things. This is just part of what it means to be an artist; you never reach a comfortable place where you can simply repeat yourself, nor do you find the perfect audience, eager to accept anything you do, even if it's quite different from what you've done in the past. The only way out of this dilemma is that every time you write a book, a story, or an article, you must do the best job you can, and prove yourself anew—like all creative writers.

Finding a New Publisher

As with everything else, there is a certain etiquette to be followed in the publishing industry. Publishers like to find successful writers and build careers with them. If you've written another book, should you stick with your current publisher or seek out another?

When to Stay

Often, publishers want to see how well your first book sells before taking on any more of your work. If your editor tells you to hold off on sending more material until sales figures from your first book start rolling in, you may be tempted to search for a new publisher. But you should resist this impulse.

Just because a publisher is hesitant to take on another book doesn't mean it won't. Having a good author–publisher relationship is important to your career. Choosing to submit your work to another publisher before showing it to your current publisher could damage that relationship. It's quite likely your editor expects to see more of your work. If your next book fits in with the current publisher's needs, it is common courtesy to first offer it to your acquisitions editor.

When to Go

Of course, there are instances in which it would be best to search for a new publisher. If your first book didn't sell well and your current publisher does not want to publish any of your other books, then by all means look elsewhere. Your next book may do well with a different publisher.

If for some reason your relationship with the acquisitions editor starts to go downhill, you should cut those ties before it gets ugly. Or maybe the relationship itself isn't bad, but you and the editor have differing views and opinions on what course your next book should take and can't come up with a compromise. If you feel as though you must sacrifice your writing to please an editor, reconsider working with that editor. In most cases, leaving a poor editor–author relationship will be a relief to the editor as well, so don't let guilt overwhelm you. But be careful, because your contract may have an options clause, which requires you to give the first consideration of your next work to your current publisher.

Exploring New Areas

If you have written a picture book, this doesn't suddenly brand you as a picture book writer. Now, whether you *want* to establish yourself as a picture book writer is a different story. You may receive advice telling you to continue writing picture books until you have established yourself in the industry. On the other hand, you may receive advice telling you to write whatever you want; your enthusiasm for the book will show through in your writing. So what should you do for your next book?

The Options

Let's say your picture book is currently going through the production process. You have been working on a young adult historical novel. However, a member of your writers' group tells you that you should write another picture book instead and make a name for yourself before plunging into other areas of children's writing. This is a message you have heard from your agent as well. Once you have proven your writing abilities to one publisher, it will be easier to do the same with another if you stay within the same genre. Besides, you don't want to be one of those authors who try their hands at writing everything under the sun only to give the appearance of being unsure of their abilities and not willing to perfect their work in one area.

Just when you are convinced, another person in your writers' group chimes in with a different opinion and makes you think again. The other member is adamant in her belief that if you write what you want to write, the joy you have in your work will show itself in the quality of your story. Just because you were successful with a picture book doesn't mean that you can't be just as successful with a young adult novel. If you force yourself to write a picture book when you want to write something else, your heart won't be in the project, and the work will reflect this.

The Decision

The decision isn't an easy one. You want to build a career as a writer, yet you don't want to sacrifice your writing and ideas to the cause. Unfortunately there isn't a right or wrong answer here. You must make the decision on your own.

If you write with the sole intention of getting your work published and into the hands of children, maybe you should follow the first writer's advice. If you write simply for the sake of writing, you should probably go with the second writer's advice. If you have both motivations (most writers do), you might plan to develop a solid reputation in one area first, then expand your reputation.

ESSENTIAL

If you do write several books in the same marketing category, you will boost your chances to become known with readers, and to gain more support and publicity from your publisher. Perhaps you should do that first, at least with your current publisher, while working on a different kind of book in (temporary) secrecy.

Writing for Magazines

While this book has focused on the writing and publication of children's books, this isn't the only area open to you if you enjoy writing for children. You may also want to consider writing for magazines. A lot of writers break into book publishing by first adding credits to their names through magazines. Some find it rewarding to write for both books and magazines. And others simply prefer the magazine style.

If you haven't already done so, check out the different children's magazines available. Just type "children's magazines" into any online search engine and you'll find that there are many out there. Some are geared toward a general audience, others are targeted to specific groups, such as preschoolers, boys who like to play hockey, and so on. All sorts of topics are covered in children's magazines. If you have researched material for a book, consider using some of it to write and sell a magazine article. If your book on this topic is being published, an article for children is an excellent way to bring you and your book to the attention of readers.

Magazines have their own styles and guidelines for written material. If you aren't familiar with writing magazine articles, you'll probably find you have a few things to learn about the form. For one thing, you usually have to write within a specified word count. This can be quite a challenge; it's a bit like solving a puzzle. After some practice, you may enjoy the exercise, and it will give you greater mastery of your craft.

Magazines have their own submission guidelines and pay rates. Just as you would follow a book publisher's guidelines to the letter, you should do the same with magazine publishers. Magazines normally pay per word or per article. If you become a proficient magazine writer, you may find that you make a better living through magazine publication than book publication.

Teaching Creative Writing

Many published writers seek a source of income in a related field. Those who thrive on social interaction and are confident in their abilities may choose to teach a class in creative writing. You could explore this by offering a free writing workshop for children in an after-school program; if you'd like to teach adults, start with a free evening class at your local library. From these first steps, you might decide to pursue a career in teaching creative writing.

ESSENTIAL

Teaching creative writing is demanding yet exhilarating. You'll discover that you always learn from your students. There are career opportunities ranging from courses in creative writing taught by certified teachers in public and private schools to university courses taught by writers with well-reviewed books and advanced degrees in the subject. Each area has its own requirements.

A Teacher's Challenge

Teaching requires a lot of hard work and preparation. It is quite different from the work of writing, and can drain creative energy from your own work. How do so many people manage to be productive writers, full-time teachers, and maintain families as well? For one thing, teachers have long vacations every year. Also, while teaching a class can be very challenging and stressful, it is also a wonderful experience. You are teaching others about a craft you love, inspiring them to become great writers for children, and thus reaching children in an indirect way. You will also discover a lot through your students, making your teaching experience a learning experience as well.

Giving Private Classes

Suppose you have published at least one book, attended writers' groups, workshops, or university courses, and feel that you are ready to try teaching. You could offer individual classes, or a series of workshops, to teens or adults. These would be independent of any school, so your qualifications would be whatever attracts students. You'll need a place to do this. You might get free space to hold classes in a library, a school, a church, a bookstore, or even a coffee shop. Think of what the owners of the venue have to gain from your activity, then discuss it with them.

Teaching a Workshop

Workshops work well with about six to twelve students, enough to bring good energy to the discussion but not so many that people are intimidated about sharing their often quite personal work. In one session of two hours, you can cover the stories of two or three people. Ideally, these will have been made available beforehand, and everyone will have read them. But in the real world, the writers will probably pass out copies of stories about ten pages long, and the group will be given ten minutes or so to read them. Another approach is to have the writer—or a designated person—read the story aloud.

Next, go around the room and let anyone who wishes to speak make comments, with this important rule: they must be honest but positive comments. You are in charge, so make sure no one person talks too long, or violates the positive feedback rule. Keep your eye on the clock. So far, the writer is not allowed to speak.

Next, go around the room again, this time in the opposite direction, and allow people to make constructive suggestions for the story. As the teacher, you should join in with articulate, specific suggestions for story improvements. This is a key part of being a good creative writing teacher—being able to give people detailed suggestions that have the ring of truth to them. Unlike teaching literature or physics, it's not just a matter of knowing the issues. Just as writing is an art that includes revision, revising the work of others is an art as well. Don't worry, though. Nobody is a master teacher on his first day.

Remember that, in your role as creative writing teacher, your primary mission is to combine kindness with honesty. You must apply this not only to your comments to students, but in your management of your class. Make sure others are tactful and constructive.

ALERT

If you like the idea of a workshop but aren't comfortable handling it on your own, consider asking other writers or editors in your area to help you organize and lead the event. This will give participants at least two different styles and views from which to learn. And if you are able to bring in someone from the publishing industry, the participants will be able to learn about both writing and publishing.

You may be wondering when the writer gets a chance to respond to all this criticism, well-meant though it may be. After everyone, including you, has weighed in, finally the writer gets to speak—but only briefly, perhaps for one minute, timed on the clock. The reason for this is that if a writer gets to gab on in response to a critique, he will be tempted to justify his choices, and to defend his work against the suggestions rather than be motivated to fix his story.

If you follow this format, you will please your students and you'll become more articulate about stories all the time. This will in turn strengthen your own writing.

Remember to keep your group small, read the work carefully ahead of time (if possible), only allow positive comments first, and keep your eye on the clock. Leave each writer with the sense that his work has been appreciated.

Teaching Creative Writing in K–12 Schools

If you are already a teacher, or planning to become certified, you may want to explore becoming certified as a creative writing teacher. There are specific courses you must take, although every state has different teaching requirements. Whether you are a published author will not matter to most schools, although it will certainly give you a leg up over other candidates for the same position. No matter how much you learn in your certification courses, remember the workshop principles discussed above, especially the part about how honest praise must come before honest criticism.

FACT

Schools sometimes bring in guest writers to teach a class to students. In good economic times, they have budgets for this that they must spend on some writer—so why not on you? For information on programs in your state, search "writers in the schools" online.

Teaching Creative Writing in a University

Creative writing has become a popular course of study in the United States at both undergraduate and graduate levels. In order to teach at this level, you would need three things: a graduate degree (usually a master of fine arts—MFA—rather than an MA), at least one book with favorable reviews, and teaching experience. The market for teaching at this level is highly competitive. In recent years the number of MFA programs, both residency and brief-residency ones, has expanded dramatically. Because there are so many, there are far more graduates each year than jobs available.

Most creative writing teaching jobs are offered to adjunct professors, part-time employees who work without benefits or job security. About a quarter of the positions available are tenure track. This means that after six years in the job you undergo a rigorous evaluation process. If you have excelled at teaching, publishing, professional activities (such as giving readings of your work at conferences), and university service (including lots of committee work), you may be granted tenure and promotion. To achieve this in most universities you will also need to have published more than one book.

If you are interested in finding out more, subscribe to The Association of Writers and Writing Programs, or AWP. Visit their website (*www.awpwriter .org*) to learn about their history and the services they offer to writers, and after you join you'll receive a password to read their excellent magazine, *The Chronicle*. This magazine is the place to learn about graduate programs, grants and awards, and job openings. The website also has a free guide that allows you to search for specific programs that meet your needs, including those which offer a specialization in writing for children and young adults.

Accepting that You Are a Writer

Many people hesitate to call themselves writers before they are published—or even after they're published, for that matter. Once you take on the title, responsibilities suddenly swoop in. You have to write and find a publisher. You have to devote time and energy to your craft when there are a thousand other things you could be doing. Creative writing is a solitary activity, and every writer seeks a proper balance between the quiet struggle to tell a good story, and the sharing of that story with others. Your satisfactions will come from thinking, researching, writing, and revising; they will come from the excitement of seeking publication; and they will come from sharing your interests in good books and the craft of writing with fellow writers, teachers, students, and children. We wish you happiness in this good work.

Resources

Further Reading

An Author's Guide to Children's Book Promotion by Susan Salzman Raab.

A Basic Guide to Writing, Selling, and Promoting Children's Books: Plus Information about Self-Publishing by Betsy B. Lee.

The Business of Writing for Children: An Award-Winning Author's Tips on How to Write, Sell, and Promote Your Children's Books by Aaron Shepard.

Children's Books and Their Creators by Anita Silvey (Editor).

Children's Writer's & Illustrator's Market by Alice Pope.

The Encyclopedia of Writing and Illustrating Children's Books by Desdemona McCannon, Sue Thornton, and Yadzia Williams.

Getting Noticed on Google by Dustin Wax.

The History of Children's Literature: A Syllabus with Selected Bibliographies by Margaret Hodges.

How to Write a Children's Book and Get It Published by Barbara Seuling.

How to Write and Illustrate Children's Books and Get Them Published by Treld Pelkey Bicknell and Felicity Trotman (Consultant Editors).

How to Write and Sell Children's Picture Books by Jean E. Karl.

It's a Bunny-Eat-Bunny World by Olga Litowinsky.

Origins of Story: On Writing for Children by Barbara Harrison and Gregory Maguire (Editors).

A Sense of Wonder: On Reading and Writing Books for Children by Katherine Paterson.

Ten Steps to Publishing Children's Books: How to Develop, Revise & Sell All Kinds of Books for Children by Berthe Amoss and Eric Suben.

The Way to Write for Children by Joan Aiken.

The Writer's Guide to Crafting Stories for Children by Nancy Lamb.

Writer's Handbook 2002 by Elfrieda Abbe (Editor).

Writing Books for Kids and Teens by Marion Crook.

Writing Books for Young People by James Cross Giblin.

Writing a Children's Book: How to Write for Children and Get Published by Pamela Cleaver.

Writing for Children by Catherine Woolley.

Writing for Children and Teenagers by Lee Wyndham.

Writing with Pictures: How to Write and Illustrate Children's Books by Uri Shulevitz.

You Can Write Children's Books by Tracey E. Dils.

Young at Heart: The Step-by-Step Way of Writing Children's Stories by Violet Ramos.

Websites

The Association of Writers and Writing Programs
www.awpwriter.org

Booklist
www.ala.org/booklist

Bookwire
www.bookwire.com

The Children's Literature Web Guide
www.ucalgary.ca/~dkbrown

Children's Writer
www.childrenswriter.com

The Children's Writing Supersite
www.write4kids.com

The Horn Book, Inc.
www.hbook.com

Literary Market Place
www.literarymarketplace.com

Publishers Weekly
www.publishersweekly.com

Purple Crayon
www.underdown.org

School Library Journal
www.slj.com

Writer's Digest
www.writersdigest.com

Organizations

American Booksellers Association
200 White Plains Road
Suite 600
Tarrytown, NY 10591
800-637-0037
www.ambook.org

American Library Association
50 East Huron
Chicago, IL 60611
800-545-2433
www.ala.org

Association of Authors' Representatives
P.O. Box 237201
Ansonia Station
New York, NY 10003
212-353-3709
www.aar-online.org

The Authors Guild
31 East 28th Street
10th Floor
New York, NY 10016
212-563-5904
www.authorsguild.org

The Children's Book Council
12 West 37th Street
2nd Floor
New York, NY 10018
212-966-1990
www.cbcbooks.org

Children's Literature Association
P.O. Box 138
Battle Creek, MI 49016
269-965-8180
www.childlitassn.org

The Institute of Children's Literature
93 Long Ridge
West Redding, CT 06896
203-792-8600
www.institutechildrenslit.com

National Center for Children's Illustrated Literature
102 Cedar
Abilene, TX 79601
325-673-4586
www.nccil.org

National Writers Union

National Office East
256 West 38th Street
Suite 703
New York, NY 10018
212-254-0279
www.nwu.org

Society of Children's Book Writers and Illustrators

8271 Beverly Boulevard
Los Angeles, CA 90048
323-782-1010
www.scbwi.org

Children's Book Publishers

The following is a list of children's publishing companies to help you get started in your search for the perfect publisher. As always, be sure to conduct your own research and verify the company name, contact information, and submission guidelines, since the industry is constantly changing. A company's website is a good place to get the needed information; however, you may find other resources such as the *Literary Market Place* and the member listing from the Children's Book Council to be of great help.

Abbeville Press
137 Varick Street
New York, NY 10013
212-366-5585
www.abbeville.com

ABDO Publishing Company
8000 W. 78th Street, Suite 310
Edina, MN 55439
800-800-1312
www.abdopub.com

Abrams
115 West 18th Street, 6th Floor
New York, NY 10011
212-206-7715
www.abramsbooks.com

Accord Publishing Ltd.
1732 Wazee Street # 202
Denver CO 80202-1284
888-333-1676
www.andrewsmcmeel.com/accord

Advance Publishing Inc.
6950 Fulton Street
Houston, TX 77022
800-917-9630
www.advancepublishing.com

Albert Whitman & Company
250 South Northwest Highway
Suite 320
Park Ridge, IL 60068
800-255-7675
www.albertwhitman.com

Knopf Publishers
Knopf Doubleday Publishing Group
1745 Broadway, 19th Floor
New York, NY 10036
212-782-9000
www.knopf.knopfdoubleday.com

Allen A. Knoll, Publishers
200 West Victoria
Santa Barbara, CA 93101-3627
805-564-3377
www.knollpublishers.com

Atheneum Books for Young Readers
Simon and Schuster
1230 Avenue of the Americas, 4th Floor
New York, NY 10020
212-698-7200
www.simonandschuster.com

August House Publishers Inc.
3500 Piedmont Road NE, Suite 310
Atlanta, GA 30305
404-442-4420
www.augusthouse.com

Azro Press
PMB 342
1704 Llano Street B
Santa Fe, NM 87505
505-989-3272
www.azropress.com

Barefoot Books
2067 Massachusetts Avenue
Cambridge, MA 02140
617-576-0660
www.barefootbooks.com

Barron's Educational Series, Inc.
250 Wireless Boulevard
Hauppauge, NY 11788
800-645-3476
www.barronseduc.com

The Bess Press
3565 Harding Avenue
Honolulu, HI 96816
808-734-7159
www.besspress.com

Bick Publishing House
307 Neck Road
Madison, CT 06443
203-245-0073
www.bickpubhouse.com

The Blue Sky Press
557 Broadway
New York, NY 10012
212-343-6100
www.scholastic.com

Boyds Mills Press
815 Church Street
Honesdale, PA 18431
800-490-5111
www.boydsmillspress.com

Bright Ring Publishing, Inc.
P.O. Box 31338
Bellingham, WA 98228
800-480-4278
www.brightring.com

Buffalo Creek Press
P.O. Box 2424
Cleburne, TX 76033
817-610-4908
www.buffalo-creek-press.com

Candlewick Press
99 Dover Street
Somerville, MA 02144
617-661-3330
www.candlewick.com

Capstone Press
151 Good Counsel Drive
P.O. Box 669
Mankato, MN 56002
800-747-4992
www.capstone-press.com

Carolrhoda Books
241 First Avenue North
Minneapolis, MN 55401-1607
800-328-4929
www.lernerbooks.com

Cascade Pass
4223 Glencoe Avenue, Suite C-105
Marina del Rey, CA 90292
310-305-0210
www.cascadepass.com

Charlesbridge Publishing
85 Main Street
Watertown, MA 02472
617-926-0329
www.charlesbridge.com

Chelsea House Publishers
132 West 31st Street, 17th Floor
New York, NY 10001
800-678-3633
www.infobasepublishing.com

The Chicken House
557 Broadway
New York, NY 10012
212-343-6100
www.scholastic.com

Children's Book Press
965 Mission Street, Suite 425
San Francisco, CA 94103
www.childrensbookpress.org

The Child's World, Inc.
1980 Lookout Drive
Mankato, MN 55317
800-599-7323
www.childsworld.com

Christian Light Publications, Inc.
P.O. Box 1212
Harrisonburg, VA 22803-1212
800-776-0478
www.clp.org

Chronicle Books
680 Second Street
San Francisco, CA 94107
415-537-4200
www.chroniclebooks.com

Crabtree Publishing
350 Fifth Avenue, Suite 3308
New York, NY 10118
800-387-7650
www.crabtreebooks.com

Clarion Books
215 Park Avenue South
New York, NY 10003
617-351-5959
www.houghtonmifflinbooks.com/clarion

David R. Godine, Publisher
9 Hamilton Place
Boston, MA 02108
617-451-9600
www.godine.com

Clear Light Books
823 Don Diego
Santa Fe, NM 87505
800-253-2747
www.clearlightbooks.com

Dial Books for Young Readers
345 Hudson Street
New York, NY 10014
212-366-2000
www.uspenguingroup.com

Concordia Publishing House
3558 South Jefferson Avenue
St. Louis, MO 63118
314-268-1000
www.cph.org

DK Publishing, Inc.
375 Hudson Street
New York, NY 10014
646-674-4000
www.us.dk.com

Coronet Books Inc.
311 Bainbridge Street
Philadelphia, PA 19147
215-925-2762
www.coronetbooks.com

Dog-Eared Publications
P.O. Box 620863
Middleton, WI 53562
888-364-3277
www.dog-eared.com

Down East Books
P.O. Box 679
Camden, ME 04843
www.downeastbooks.com

Dutton Children's Books
345 Hudson Street
New York, NY 10014
212-366-2000
www.uspenguingroup.com

EDC Publishing
P.O. Box 470663
Tulsa, OK 74147-0663
800-475-4522
www.edcpub.com

Editorial Unilit
1360 NW 88th Avenue
Miami, FL 33172
800-767-7726
www.editorialunilit.com

Eerdmans Books for Young Readers
2140 Oak Industrial Drive NE
Grand Rapids, MI 49505
800-253-7521
www.eerdmans.com/youngreaders

Enslow Publishers, Inc.
Box 398, 40 Industrial Road, Dept. F61
Berkeley Heights, NJ 07922
800-398-2504
www.enslow.com

Evan-Moor Publishers
18 Lower Ragsdale Drive
Monterey, CA 93940
800-714-0971
www.evan-moor.com

Farrar, Straus, & Giroux Books
18 West 18th Street
New York, NY 10011
212-741-6900
www.fsgbooks.com

Free Spirit Publishing
217 Fifth Avenue North, Suite 200
Minneapolis, MN 55401
612-338-2068
www.freespirit.com

Freedom Publishing Company
2550 Crawford Avenue
Evanston, IL 60201
800-717-0770
www.freedompub.com

Front Street Books
Boyds Mills Press
815 Church Street
Honesdale, PA 18431
570-253-1164 · 800-490-5111
www.frontstreetbooks.com
or *boydsmillspress.com*

Fulcrum Publishing
4690 Table Mountain Parkway, Suite 100
Golden, CO 80403
800-992-2908
www.fulcrum-books.com

Gale Cengage Learning
27500 Drake Road
Farmington Hills, MI 48331
800-877-GALE
www.gale.cengage.com

Gallopade International
6000 Shakerag Hill, Suite 314
P.O. Box 2779
Peachtree City, GA 30269
770-631-4222
www.gallopade.com

Gareth Stevens Publishing
111 East 14th Street, Suite #349
New York, NY 10003
800-542-2595
www.garethstevens.com

Good News Crossway
1300 Crescent Street
Wheaton, IL 60187
630-682-4300
www.gnpcb.org

Greene Bark Press Inc.
P.O. Box 1108
Bridgeport, CT 06601
610-434-2802
www.greenebarkpress.com

Greenleaf Press
3761 Highway 109 North
Lebanon, TN 37087
615-449-1617
www.greenleafpress.com

Gryphon House, Inc.
10770 Columbia Pike, Suite 201
Silver Spring, MD 20901
800-638-0928
www.gryphonhouse.com

Hachai Publishing
527 Empire Boulevard
Brooklyn, NY 11225
718-633-0100
www.hachai.com

Hampton-Brown Company
26385 Carmel Rancho Boulevard
Carmel, CA 93923
831-625-3666
www.hampton-brown.com

HarperCollins Children's Books
1350 Avenue of the Americas
New York, NY 10019
212-207-7000
www.harpercollinschildrens.com

Harrison House Publishers
P.O. Box 35035
Tulsa, OK 74153
800-888-4126
www.harrisonhouse.com

Health Communications Inc.
3201 SW 15th Street
Deerfield Beach, FL 33442
800-441-5569
www.hcibooks.com

Health Press
2920 Carlisle Boulevard NE
Albuquerque, NM 87110
505-888-1394
www.healthpress.com

Heyday Books
P.O. Box 9145
Berkeley, CA 94709
510-549-3564
www.heydaybooks.com

Holiday House Inc.
425 Madison Avenue
New York, NY 10017
Fax: 212-688-0085
www.holidayhouse.com

Holy Cow! Press
P.O. Box 3170
Mount Royal Station
Duluth, MN 55803
218-724-1653
www.holycowpress.org

Houghton Mifflin Harcourt
222 Berkeley Street
Boston, MA 02116
617-351-5000
www.hmhco.com

Hyperion Books
114 Fifth Avenue
New York, NY 10011
www.hyperionbooks.com

Illumination Arts Publishing
P.O. Box 1865
Bellevue, WA 98009
425-968-5097
www.illumin.com

InnovativeKids
18 Ann Street
Norwalk, CT 06854
203-838-6400
www.innovativekids.com

Interlink Publishing Group, Inc.
46 Crosby Street
Northampton, MA 01060
800-238-LINK
www.interlinkbooks.com

Jewish Lights Publishing
P.O. Box 237
Sunset Farm Offices, Route 4
Woodstock, VT 05091
802-457-4000
www.jewishlights.com

Jewish Publication Society
2100 Arch Street, 2nd Floor
Philadelphia, PA 19103
215-832-0600
www.jewishpub.org

Jonathan David Publishers, Inc.
68-22 Eliot Avenue
Middle Village, NY 11379-1194
www.jdbooks.com

Judaica Press, Inc.
123 Ditmas Avenue
Brooklyn, NY 11218
718-972-6200
www.judaicapress.com

Kar-Ben Publishing
241 First Avenue
North Minneapolis, MN 55401
800-328-4929
www.karben.com

KAZI Publications
3023 West Belmont Avenue
Chicago, IL 60618
773-267-7001
www.kazi.org

Kids Can Press
2250 Military Road
Tonawanda, NY 14150
800-265-0884
www.kidscanpress.com/US

KTAV Publishing Inc.
930 Newark Avenue, 4th floor
Jersey City, NJ 07306
201-963-9524
www.ktav.com

Lee & Low Books
95 Madison Avenue, Suite 1205
New York, NY 10016
212-779-4400
www.leeandlow.com

Lerner Publishing Group
241 1st Avenue N
Minneapolis, MN 55401
800-328-4929
www.lernerbooks.com

Loyola Press
3441 North Ashland Avenue
Chicago, IL 60657
800-621-1008
www.loyolapress.org

Magination Press
750 First Street, NE
Washington, DC 20002
800-374-2721
www.apa.org/pubs/magination

Margaret K. McElderry Books
1230 Avenue of the Americas
New York, NY 10020
212-698-7200
www.simonandschuster.com

Marshall Cavendish Corporation
99 White Plains Road
Tarrytown, NY 10591
914-332-8888
www.marshallcavendish.us

Maval Publishing Inc.
3900 East 6th Avenue
Denver, CO 80206
866-418-0960
www.mavalpublishing.com

May Davenport Publishers
26313 Purissima Road
Los Altos Hills, CA 94022
650-947-1275
www.maydavenportpublishers.com

McGraw-Hill Children's Publishing
Two Penn Plaza, 11th Floor
New York, NY 10121-2298
212-512-2000
www.mhschool.com

Meadowbrook Press
5451 Smetana Drive
Minnetonka, MN 55343
800-338-2232
www.meadowbrookpress.com

Milkweed Editions
1011 Washington Avenue South
Suite 300
Minneapolis, MN 55415-1246
612-332-3192
www.milkweed.org

The Millbrook Press
2 Old New Milford Road
Brookfield, CT 06804
203-740-2220
www.lernerbooks.com

Mondo Publishing Inc.
980 Avenue of the Americas
New York, NY 10018
888-886-6636
www.mondopub.com

Morgan Reynolds Publishers
620 South Elm Street, Suite 223
Greensboro, NC 27406
800-535-1504
www.morganreynolds.com

Morning Glory Press
6595 San Haroldo Way
Buena Park, CA 90620
888-612-8254
www.morningglorypress.com

New World Library
14 Pamaron Way
Novato, CA 94949
800-972-6657
www.newworldlibrary.com

National Geographic Children's Books
1145 17th Street NW
Washington, DC 20036
877-873-6846
www.ngchildrensbooks.org

New Canaan Publishing Company
2384 N Hwy 341
Rossville, GA 30741
423-285-8672
www.newcanaanpublishing.com

Newmarket Press
18 East 48th Street
New York, NY 10017
212-832-3575
www.newmarketpress.com

North-South Books
350 Seventh Avenue, Suite 1400
New York, NY 10010
212-706-4545
www.northsouth.com

The Oliver Press, Inc.
Charlotte Square
5707 West 36th Street
Minneapolis, MN 55416
952-926-8981
www.oliverpress.com

Open Hand Publishing, LLC
P.O. Box 20207
Greensboro, NC 27420
336-292-8585
www.openhand.com

Orca Book Publishers
P.O. Box 468
Custer, WA 98240
800-210-5277
www.orcabook.com

The Overmountain Press
P.O. Box 1261
Johnson City, TN 37605
423-926-2691
www.overmtn.com

Paintbox Press
208 Glandon Drive
Chapel Hill, NC 27514
919-969-7512
www.paintboxpress.com

Parachute Publishing, LLC
156 Fifth Avenue, Suite 302
New York, NY 10010
212-691-1422
www.parachutepublishing.com

Parkway Publishers, Inc.
P.O. Box 3678
Boone, NC 28607
828-265-3993
www.parkwaypublishers.com

Patria Press, Inc.
4635 Statesmen Drive
Indianapolis, IN 46250
317-577-1321
www.patriapress.com

Pearson Learning Group
135 South Mount Zion Road
P.O. Box 2500
Lebanon, IN 46052
800-526-9907
www.pearsonschool.com

Pelican Publishing Company, Inc.
1000 Burmaster Street
Gretna, LA 70053
800-843-1724
www.pelicanpub.com

Perfection Learning
100 North Second Avenue
Logan, IA 51546
800-831-4190
www.perfectionlearning.com

Platypus Media
725 8th Street, SE
Washington, DC 20003
202-752-8977
www.platypusmedia.com

Pleasant Company Publications
American Girl
P.O. Box 620497
Middleton, WI 53562-0497
800-360-1861
www.americangirlpublishing.com

Polychrome Publishing Corporation
4509 North Francisco
Chicago, IL 60625
www.polychromebooks.com

Pro Lingua Press
P.O. Box 24368
Los Angeles, CA 90024
310-472-8396
www.prolinguapress.com

Prometheus Books
59 John Glenn Drive
Amherst, NY 14228
800-421-0351
www.prometheusbooks.com

Providence House Publishers
238 Seaboard Lane
Franklin, TN 37067
800-321-5692
www.providencehouse.com

Puffin Books
345 Hudson Street, 15th Floor
New York, NY 10014
212-366-2795
www.uspenguingroup.com

Random House Young Readers Group
1540 Broadway
New York, NY 10036
212-782-9000
www.randomhouse.com/kids

RDR Books
1487 Glen Avenue
Muskegon, MI 49441
510-595-0595
www.rdrbooks.com

Reader's Digest Children's Publishing
480 Bedford Road
Pleasantville, NY 10570-2929
914-238-1000
www.readersdigestkids.com

Richard C. Owen Publishers, Inc.
P.O. Box 585
Katonah, NY 10536
800-336-5588
www.rcowen.com

The Rosen Publishing Group
29 East 21st Street
New York, NY 10010
800-237-9932
www.rosenpublishing.com

Running Press Book Publishers
2300 Chestnut Street, Suite 200
Philadelphia, PA 19103
215-567-5080
www.runningpress.com

William H. Sadlier, Inc.
9 Pine Street, 2nd Floor
New York, NY 10005
800-221-5175
www.sadlier.com

Sasquatch Books
119 South Main, Suite 400
Seattle, WA 98104
www.sasquatchbooks.com

Scholastic Inc.
Scholastic Professional Books
557 Broadway, 5th Floor
New York, NY 10012
212-343-6100
www.scholastic.com

School Specialty

W6316 Design Drive
Greenville, WI 54942
888-388-3224
www.schoolspecialty.com

Seedling Publications

Continental Press
520 East Bainbridge Street
Elizabethtown, PA 17022
800-233-0759
www.seedlingpub.com

The Shoe String Press, Inc.

2 Linsley Street
North Haven, CT 06473
203-239-2702
www.shoestringpress.com

Sierra Club Books

85 Second Street, 2nd Floor
San Francisco, CA 94105
415-977-5500
www.sierraclub.org/books

Silver Moon Press

400 East 85th Street
New York, NY 10028
800-874-3320
www.silvermoonpress.com

Skinner House Books

25 Beacon Street
Boston, MA 02108
617-742-2100
www.uua.org/publications/skinnerhouse

SkyLight Paths Publishing

Route 4, P.O. Box 237
Woodstock, VT 05091
802-457-4000
www.skylightpaths.com

SoftPlay, Inc.

3535 West Peterson Avenue
Chicago, IL 60659
800-515-5437
www.softplayforkids.com

Stemmer House Publishers, Inc.

P.O. Box 89
4 White Brook Road
Gilsum, NH 03448
800-345-6665
www.stemmer.com

Sterling Publishing Company, Inc.

387 Park Avenue South, 11th Floor
New York, NY 10016-8810
www.sterlingpub.com

Sundance Publishing
33 Boston Post Road West, Suite 440
Marlborough, MA 01752
800-343-8204
www.sundancepub.com

Torah Aura Productions
4423 Fruitland Avenue
Los Angeles, CA 90058
800-238-6724
www.torahaura.com

Tricycle Press
The Crown Publishing Group
2625 Alcatraz Avenue, P.O. Box 505
Berkeley, CA 94705
510-285-3000
www.tricycle.crownpublishing.com

Trident Press International
The Crown Publishing Group
801 12th Avenue South, Suite 400
Naples, FL 34102
239-649-7077
www.trident-international.com

Tundra Books
P.O. Box 1030
Plattsburgh, NY 12901
800-788-1074
www.tundrabooks.com

Tyndale House Publishers
351 Executive Drive
Carol Stream, IL 60188
800-323-9400
www.tyndale.com

UAHC Press
633 Third Avenue, 7th Floor
New York, NY 10017-6778
212-650-4120
www.uahcpress.com

Underwood Books
P.O. Box 1919
Nevada City, CA 95959
www.underwoodbooks.com

Viking Children's Books
345 Hudson Street
New York, NY 10014
212-366-2000
www.us.penguingroup.com

Volcano Press
P.O. Box 270
Volcano, CA 95689-0270
800-879-9636
www.volcanopress.com

VSP Books Inc.
14807 Build America Drive
Woodbridge, VA 22191
703-910-6683
www.vspbooks.com

Walker and Company
175 Fifth Avenue
New York, NY 10010
www.walkerbooks.com

Walter Foster Publishing
3 Wrigley, Suite A
Irvine, CA 92618
800-426-0099
www.walterfoster.com

WaterBrook Multnomah Publishing Group
12265 Oracle Boulevard. Suite 200
Colorado Springs, CO 80921
719-590-4999
www.waterbrookmultnomah.com

Western New York Wares Inc.
P.O. Box 733
Ellicott Station
Buffalo, NY 14205
www.wnybooks.com

W.H. Freeman & Company
41 Madison Avenue, 37th Floor
New York, NY 10010
800-903-3019
www.whfreeman.com

Winslowpress
Editorial, Sales and Marketing
36 West 20th Street, Third Floor
New York, NY 10010
212-366-4160
www.winslowpress.com

Woodbine House
6510 Bells Mill Road
Bethesda, MD 20817
800-843-7323
www.woodbinehouse.com

Workman Publishing Company
225 Varick Street
New York, NY 10014-4381
212-254-5900
www.workman.com

Wright Group/McGraw-Hill Education
130 E. Randolph, 4th Floor
Chicago, IL 60601
312-233-6520
www.mheonline.com

YWAM Publishing
P.O. Box 55787
Seattle, WA 98155
800-922-2143
www.ywampublishing.com

Zondervan Publishing
5300 Patterson SE
Grand Rapids, MI 49530
800-727-3480
www.zondervan.com

Index

We Have EVERYTHING® on Anything!

With more than 19 million copies sold, the Everything® series has become one of America's favorite resources for solving problems, learning new skills, and organizing lives. Our brand is not only recognizable—it's also welcomed.

The series is a hand-in-hand partner for people who are ready to tackle new subjects—like you!

For more information on the Everything® series, please visit *www.adamsmedia.com*

The Everything® list spans a wide range of subjects, with more than 500 titles covering 25 different categories:

Business	History	Reference
Careers	Home Improvement	Religion
Children's Storybooks	Everything Kids	Self-Help
Computers	Languages	Sports & Fitness
Cooking	Music	Travel
Crafts and Hobbies	New Age	Wedding
Education/Schools	Parenting	Writing
Games and Puzzles	Personal Finance	
Health	Pets	